GORDON MEMORIAL LIBRARY

3GORL00019422N

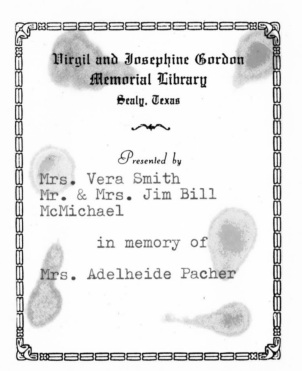

**Virgil and Josephine Gordon
Memorial Library**
Sealy, Texas

Presented by

Mrs. Vera Smith
Mr. & Mrs. Jim Bill
McMichael

in memory of

Mrs. Adelheide Pacher

D1224255

VIRGIL AND JOSEPHINE GORDON
MEMORIAL LIBRARY
917 North Circle Drive
SEALY, TEXAS 77474

VIRGIL AND JOSEPHINE GORDON
MEMORIAL LIBRARY

TEXAS WOMEN

A PICTORIAL HISTORY

From Indians to Astronauts

Ruthe Winegarten

EAKIN PRESS
Austin, Texas

VIRGIL AND JOSEPHINE GORDON
MEMORIAL LIBRARY
917 North Circle Drive
SEALY, TEXAS 77474

FIRST EDITION

Copyright ©
By Ruthe Winegarten

Published in the United States of America
By Eakin Press, P.O. Box 23066, Austin, Texas 78735

ALL RIGHTS RESERVED. No part of this book may be reproduced in any form without written permission from the publisher, except for brief passages included in a review appearing in a newspaper or magazine.

ISBN 0-89015-532-1

Contents

Foreword

As you peruse *Texas Women: A Pictorial History*, think about the women who gaze out at you from their serious, often grim portraits.

What do you see?

Do you see the grit that allowed them to endure, even thrive in our rough, frontier existence?

Do you see the character and determination that went into the building of our communities and our state?

Do you see the pride that went into the making of loving homes for their families?

Do you see the spirit that allowed these women to persevere and achieve?

Well, it's there. And as you study these faces and places of our past, you will see more. You may even be moved. Some of these women may touch you with their courage, daring, and tenacity. Some may touch you with their longings and frustrations. And some may touch you because of their very anonymity and obscurity.

Brought together for the first time in book format by historian Ruthe Winegarten, these visual reminders will give you a hint of what Texas was like for the forgotten half of its population — the women.

And what a reminder! Texas women built communities, started schools, founded churches, funded museums, created libraries, set up hospitals, ran ranches, preserved public monuments, built parks, influenced government, served in public office, wrote books, starred in movies, worked in factories, set up businesses, developed products, endured hardship, suffered loneliness, nursed the sick, helped the helpless, experienced love, gave birth and values to children, and more. In short, Texas women experienced life! And they engaged in activities, both public and private, that made the experience of life richer for others.

Our tragedy as a people has been that until recently we have neither known nor recognized the value of the role of women in our history.

That is changing.

Texas Women: A Pictorial History is the most recent addition to a growing body of work about women in Texas history. It is a trend I hope will continue.

Before the development of the touring exhibition *Texas Women: A Celebration of History* in 1981 and the legacy of its research files, now located at Texas Woman's University in Denton, there were few hints that Texas women even had a history.

When the Texas Foundation for Women's Resources, the exhibition sponsor, decided that the history of Texas women was worth discovering and telling, there was no logical place where a researcher could find general information about the heritage of Texas women. Materials and references were scattered all across the state. Boxes of primary source material belonging to women — diaries, letters, legal documents and artifacts — were often stored unlabeled in library basements or museum storerooms. There was no index to these kinds of materials, no central catalogue, no bibliography of sources. In short, no one knew what — if anything — existed that could document the history of women in Texas.

Researchers for the exhibition had to identify many of these records and to help professional historians see their value. They compiled information on more than 200 topics relating to women's roles. They included everything from a statistical analysis of women's work in Texas to the history of midwives. In addition, they collected biographical information on almost 600 women. They built files on the famous and the not-so-famous. Again, the files included everything from newspaper clippings, letters, and unpublished thesis material to personal interviews with the individual woman or her surviving relatives.

When Ruthe Winegarten worked on the original exhibition, she compiled a bibliography of more than 2,000 sources on women's history in Texas. And after the exhibition, she also edited for Texas Woman's University a Finders Guide to the files.

In the process of her research and cataloguing, Winegarten came across enough stories and photographs about remarkable women to constitute a dozen exhibitions. The women and their images were too compelling to leave alone. But there was simply not enough room for all of the photographs in the original exhibit. So, we talked about saving the stories and photographs for a separate pictorial history in book form.

Now almost five years after the opening of the museum exhibition, Winegarten has fulfilled her dream. And we are indebted to her because she is presenting to Texas women the gift of their rediscovered heritage. These photographs make women visible. As such, they help place value upon the many activities of women, which have had very little public recognition or respect. It is a gift evoking feelings somewhat like a lonely orphan might feel if she were to discover suddenly that she were part of a warm, loving, and respectable family that welcomed her into their home. It is the feeling of finally belonging and being a valued member of society.

This kind of feeling is explosive. It instills self-confidence and a feeling of self-worth. It allows women to take the risks necessary for public or private leadership. And that leadership, plus skills, intelligence and hard work, can allow women to try anything they want in our society with some hope of success.

Please remember that as you peruse *Texas Women: A Pictorial History*. It is more than a book of pictures.

— MARY BETH ROGERS
Deputy Treasurer, State of Texas
Former Director, Texas Women's
History Project

Preface

This book was designed as a guide and blueprint for historians, teachers, students, librarians, parents, writers, and others interested in Texas history. It is part of a continuing process of discovering and documenting the activities and achievements of women in Texas's history.

Texas is more than just its wars, and its cowboys, and its oil wells. The achievements of Texas women, as individuals and through their organizations, have been omitted, for the most part, from Texas history books. The history of Texas is the history of the growth of a society, a large-scale multi-ethnic one, full of people and communities, politics and culture, quiet interludes, and more than a little dazzle and glitter. We are still learning about the full sweep of that history, but none of us can know it completely until we look closely at all the material available to us — namely, information about one-half the people of the state — the women. One of the major components of this book concerns the role women have played as workers, community builders, and as creators — not only of children, but of the institutions which make a society civilized.

Texas women have built tepees and founded cities, done housework and field work, and labored without pay as slaves. They have worked for pay in offices, homes, on farms, and in factories. They have owned and managed small businesses and large corporations. They have taught school and practiced law and medicine. They have enriched society with their art, literature, music, and handwork. And as wives, mothers, and single women, they have cared for their children and those of others.

Almost all Texas women, regardless of ethnic or class differences, have shared many experiences — motherhood, family care, healing, hard work, and community building. Within the context of those experiences, women have often reached out to each other across invisible barriers to work together. These efforts and successes have strengthened Texas. Each ethnic group, however, has its distinctive story, and these separate threads form part of the entire fabric.

Women's achievements have been recorded in practically all fields and symbolized by outstanding individuals. Texas women ran the fastest and flew the farthest and walked in space — they were gunrunners and peacemakers, laundresses, and spies, judges, ranchers, bakers and bridge builders. This book includes many of them. It also includes the stories of many women who banded together in missionary societies, clubs, and powerful organized groups to improve their own status and that of their communities and state. They got together to improve public education and sanitation, create schools, hospitals, churches and synagogues, symphony orchestras, and museums, and gardens along the highways. They lobbied for child labor laws, pure food and drug laws, prison reform, and the vote. They protected family life by protesting lynching and providing shelter for battered women.

This book presents the lives and work, not of all women, but of a representative sampling of women and their organizations and their activities. Much more research is required to write a comprehensive history of Texas women. The historian, the scholar, the student, and the concerned citizen can contribute to this process through further research and writing.

— Ruthe Winegarten

November 1985

Acknowledgments

This book is an outgrowth of the Texas Women's History Project which was sponsored by the Texas Foundation for Women's Resources. It is based in large part on the research conducted by the staff in preparation for the exhibit, "Texas Women, a Celebration of History," the files, and the publications which grew out of that project.

I wish to acknowledge the outstanding staff members and consultants whose insights, detective work, and persistence have made a lasting contribution to the field of Texas women's history. They are Mary Beth Rogers, the Project Director; and Cynthia Beeman, Dr. Rose Brewer, Dr. Evey Chapa, Martha Cotera, Nancy Fleming, Melissa Hield, Mary Sanger, Janelle Scott, Sherry A. Smith, Ellen C. Temple, and Frieda Werden.

Preliminary design for this book was done by Sherry A. Smith. Invaluable editorial advice and assistance were given by Frieda Werden and Dr. Stanley Schneider. Linda Webster's good humor and dedication in turning the manuscript into the finished product was essential. Shirley Ratisseau's editorial judgment and expertise were greatly appreciated.

For photographic assistance, I am indebted in particular to the following: Tom Shelton, Institute of Texan Cultures, UT-San Antonio; Ralph Elder, Barker Texas History Center, UT-Austin; Joy Hudon, Texas/Dallas Public Library; Austin History Center (Austin Public Library); Ellen Kuniyaki Brown, Texas Collection, Baylor University, Waco; Gina McNeely, Austin; Cynthia Beeman, Texas State Archives; Metta Nicewarner, Special Collections, Texas Woman's University, Denton; and the Humanities Research Center, UT-Austin.

To the lost women and the found women
Our mothers and grandmothers
Sisters and daughters
Aunts and cousins
Nieces and neighbors
Friends and colleagues
Those who nurtured us
And whom we have nurtured.

For the thing that bound them together was not a chain
Not a chain but a vision
Not a chain, but the women:
As stars consider each other,
The search for the women is song.
— Frieda Werden

A Wichita woman. Wichitas were a North Central Texas tribe who farmed and lived in permanent settlements of grass huts. Wichita Falls preserves their name.

1

PIONEERS

Native Americans were the first Texans. For at least 10,000 years, hundreds of tribes developed complex societies, languages, and cultures. Women were central to the economic and social life of all tribes, and many held important ritual and decision-making roles. The labor of Native American women was essential to tribal survival. Wichita and Caddo women farmed; Comanches and Kiowas butchered bison and tanned hides; Jumano women made baskets and pottery; and Tonkawas cured and roasted meat. All women were responsible for cooking and child care, and many were healers.

The Spanish settled Texas with missions, presidios, and haciendas in the 1600s and 1700s. Hispanic and Native American women accompanied Spanish soldier-husbands as cooks, laundresses, and gardeners. Intermarriage and mingling, sometimes forced, among Spanish, Native Americans, and Mestizos, produced children of mixed ancestry. Also, many Amerindians converted to Catholicism and subsequently adopted Spanish surnames and life-styles, thus obscuring their roots. The missions ultimately failed because Native Americans died of European diseases, resisted mission labor and religion, and ran away or rebelled.

The Spaniards brought their language, culture, and concepts of individual land ownership and community property from Europe to Texas. These concepts and laws enabled Hispanic women to be among the earliest landowners in the region. Some had land grants in their own names; others inherited from husbands and fathers. While a few Hispanic women had large ranches and were influential, most were poor and anonymous; but their labor — as wives, mothers, farmers, seamstresses, shopkeepers, potters—was absolutely vital.

Once Stephen F. Austin opened the door to widespread North American and slave immigration in the 1820s, white women of all social and economic classes came to Texas — as newlyweds, with their families, or sometimes as single women or widows. They came in wagons and in ships, from the Deep South, trans-Appalachia, Europe, and New England. Initially they settled along the Gulf Coast and in East and Central Texas — in towns, on small farms, and on large plantations. Slaves came to Texas along with the immigrants, but most white families had no slaves.

Slavery was profitable for many slave owners, but sometimes devastating for slave women. They worked endless hours in fields and houses, doing farm labor, domestic work, and skilled production such as spinning and weaving. Some were subjected to frequent violence and the splitting of families; many resisted by running away, breaking tools, or even poisoning their owners.

Not all blacks were slaves. Some free women of color were Texas pioneers. A few owned land, and others hired out as nurses, laundresses, and domestics. When the Republic of Texas legalized slavery in 1840, it became illegal for people of color to remain in the state and stay free. A number of women of color petitioned for the right to remain as free citizens. Most petitions were ignored or denied —but a few were granted.

Throughout the years of settlement, there was bloodshed and violence between cultures. Women participated on all sides of these wars — as nurses, cooks, laundresses, wives and mothers, and camp followers; as victims and captives; and sometimes as fighters and spies. However, many women wished for peace and stability, and at times they expressed understanding across cultural lines.

"The women work very hard, and do a great deal; of the twenty-four hours they have only six of repose."
—*Cabeza de Vaca, 1542*

PREPARING A BUFFALO HIDE

A team of Native American women could butcher three buffalo in one day. Dressing a buffalo hide took three days of very hard work. Great skill was needed to turn a hide into leather for tepee covers and clothing. The women used their handmade tools to scrape hair and fat from the skins, then softened them by rubbing, and waterproofed them with bear or buffalo grease.

4

NATIVE AMERICAN WOMEN WERE TEXAS'S FIRST ARCHITECTS, ENGINEERS, AND CONSTRUCTION WORKERS

Amerindian women were among Texas's earliest home builders. Their tepees were ingeniously designed to generate winter warmth and summer coolness. In winter the open space around the bottom was chinked with grass or animal skins for weatherproofing, and in summer the lower part of the tepee cover was raised.

Tepees were stable in strong winds; the center pole served as an anchor which the wind drove deeper into the ground. Movable skin flaps regulated the air flow, and smoke escaped through the top.

Native American Women Could Pack and Move Their Camp Very Quickly.

The squaws packed all the movable articles ... in large bundles of untanned buffalo skins. These they carried to the river, set upon each one a pair of black-eyed papooses and propelled the bundles over the swift, swollen stream to the opposite shore with the greatest dexterity. Two squaws always swam near a bundle. . . .

They carried the bundles up the high bank with great exertion but always in the best spirits. ... The men did not participate in this work, but primped and decorated themselves. ... Later the squaws drove the rest of their many horses across the stream, and in a short time the trans-

fer of the camp was accomplished. In the evening some of the men came to town in full war regalia.
— Ferdinand Roemer, *Texas*, 1849

It took strong women working together to construct the 300-pound tepees. They used twenty poles covered with fifteen buffalo skins they had hand sewn.

Comanche women moved their children and all the tribe's possessions, including their tepees, on two trailing poles called a travois roped to their two-horned work saddles.

"She is like a queen among them."
—*Fray Gaspar José de Solís, 1767–1768
writing about Santa Adiva*

translating for the Spanish and French and promoting Christianity. Angelina County, the only one named for a woman, honors her.

There are at least six references to Angelina or a woman fitting her description in the records of explorers and missionaries. In 1691, Father Massanet described an "Indian maiden with a bright intellect and possessing striking personal appearance," who "expressed a desire to learn the Father's language." In 1716, Father Isidro Felís de Espinoza wrote that his expedition had "recourse to a learned Indian woman of this Assinai [Hasinai] tribe, reared in Coahuila." Fray Francisco Celiz's diary of 1718–1719 described a "Sagacious Indian woman interpreter." Final mention is made by Fray Juan Morfí in 1721, who observed "one Angelina who has been raised on the Rio Grande and spoke both Spanish and the Texas languages" serving as interpreter.

Santa Adiva

Santa Adiva, a Caddo leader of great authority, was described by Fray Gaspar José de Solís as a "Great Lady" or "Principal Lady." "Her house is very large and has many rooms. The rest of the Nations bring presents and gifts to her. She has many Indian men and women in her service called *tamas comas*, and these are like priests and captains among them. She is married to five Indian men."

Matriarchal Tribes

Some tribes, like the matriarchal Tonkawas, Wichitas, and Caddos, were peaceful and traded with the white immigrants. The oldest competent woman, known as "mother of the house," was the director and dominant person in her family. At death her oldest daughter replaced her. A "mother of the house" might have considerable control over a son-in-law, even though he was a chief or an outstanding warrior. They considered the ideal family to be a woman, her sisters, her husband, unmarried children, and daughters and their families.

In the beginning of the world there was only one woman, and this woman had two daughters.

—Hasinai Creation Story

Wichitas believed in a number of gods and goddesses. A moon goddess—Bright Shining Woman—one of the most important figures—controlled reproduction of humans, animals, and crops. Earth Mother was believed to have given birth to everything.

Angelina was a leader of an East Texas Caddo tribe for thirty years (ca. 1690–1721).

Among the Native American tribes living in Texas when the Spanish arrived in 1528 were the matrilineal Caddos (Hasinais) of East Texas. The two women leaders whose names we know were Caddo: Angelina, a translator, and the tribal leader, Santa Adiva.

Angelina

Angelina was baptized and educated by Spanish friars at the Mission of San Juan Bautista on the Rio Grande around 1700. She returned to her tribe,

A Tonkawa woman. Tonkawas were a Central Texas matriarchal tribe.

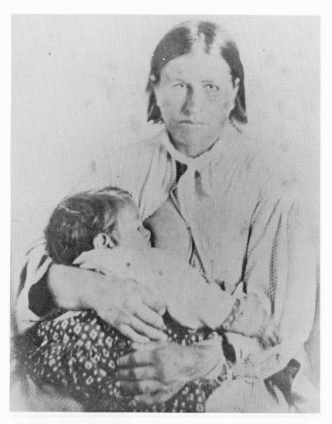

Cynthia Ann Parker (1827–1864) lived with the Comanches for twenty-four years. She and her baby Prairie Flower were recaptured by Anglos in 1860.

Cynthia Ann Parker

From the time the Spaniards, North Americans, and Europeans came to Texas, there was conflict and continuous warfare against the Native Americans. No formal war was ever declared, but the bloodshed, fear, and hostility were real, and it was war nonetheless. Women of all ethnicities suffered greatly. Many saw their children killed or kidnapped, their homes burned or looted, and their husbands, brothers, fathers, and sons killed.

Cynthia Ann Parker, the White Comanche of the Plains, was a double victim of this conflict. The child of white settlers, she had been captured in 1836, at the age of nine, and traded to a Comanche tribe. She learned to tan hide, preserve buffalo meat, and raise a tepee. She adjusted to her new life, married noted war chief Pete Nocona, bore three children, and considered herself a Comanche. She had two sons, Pecos and Quanah Parker, the Comanche's last great war chief.

Twice Cynthia Ann was seen by white men and once had turned aside offers of freedom. In 1860, Texas Rangers mistook a Comanche work party consisting of Cynthia Ann, some other women, and a

Mexican man for an entire village. The Rangers killed the man (thinking him Pete Nocona) and all the women except Cynthia Ann and her baby Prairie Flower, whom they captured. Unable to become reconciled to the almost unknown environment, Cynthia Ann tried repeatedly to escape her rescuers and rejoin her people. When Prairie Flower died, Cynthia Ann Parker slashed her breasts in mourning and grieved herself to death. She survived great hardship only to become a victim of "civilization."

Some Women Wrote Of Friendly Contacts With The Indians

Although historians have emphasized frontier hostilities, many women wrote of friendly contacts with the Native Americans and condemned their treatment by Anglo settlers. Dilue Rose Harris remembered that some "Indians did not trouble anybody. They traded baskets, moccasins embroidered with beads." Mathilda Doebbler Gruen Wagner said, "The Indians were friendly and helpful until the settlers started driving them out as though they were cattle."

Sallie Reynolds Matthews explained the reason for the Native Americans' hostility toward the whites: "If they had been treated more humanely from the beginning, there would have been much less rapine and bloodshed. What could we expect of a people that were gradually being driven from their home and country, their hunting grounds being taken without remuneration?"

Sallie Reynolds Matthews (1861–1938) condemned the treatment of Native Americans in Interwoven: A Pioneer Chronicle: *"I do think our race has much to answer for."*

Comanche families like this one were among the last Native Americans driven from Texas, rounded up and herded off to Oklahoma reservations. Many died from hunger and mistreatment. Today there are three tribal groups in Texas, the Alabama-Coushattas, the Tiguas, and the Kickapoos, and thousands of Native Americans living in urban areas.

María Jesús de Agreda

The legend of The Lady in Blue is a "tall tale" which has intrigued Texans for over 300 years.

María Jesús de Agreda was a Spanish nun and later abbess who began having spells at the age of eighteen during which she said her lifeless body was transported as if in a dream to an unknown land. She claimed to have made 500 trips from 1620 to 1631, all without having left her post in a Spanish convent.

During this period, Father Alonso de Benavides was working with the Jumanos in West Texas; he was amazed at their descriptions of a Lady in Blue who they said had taught them the Christian faith. When Father Alonso visited María in Spain in 1631, she told him of her extraordinary gift of bilocation (being in two places at one time) and of her countless trips to Texas. No natural explanation was ever given for her experiences.

Tales of her transatlantic pilgrimages were so widespread that even King Philip IV visited her. She wrote a controversial three-volume work, *The Mystical City of God and the Divine History of the Virgin Mary of God*, which was periodically on and off the Inquisitional Index.

María Jesús de Agreda (1602–1665) was a Spanish nun and missionary. She claimed to have made 500 trips to Texas, while in a trance, to preach to native tribes.

Doña Patricia (de la Garza) de León (1777–1849)

Doña Patricia de la Garza de León, a beautiful, aristocratic woman born in Mexico, was one of the earliest pioneer women to settle in Texas. She staked her $10,000 inheritance and livestock to help her husband, Empresario Don Martín, found the town of Victoria in 1824.

Doña Patricia became the richest person in Texas after Don Martín's death in 1833. She sided with the Texans in their war with Mexico and contributed large sums to the war effort. After Texas independence, anti-Mexican sentiment forced her and her family to flee. One son was murdered, and their property was confiscated or stolen. She later returned to Victoria, living very modestly.

Doña Patricia brought religion, schools, and a social and cultural life to Victoria, and the community institutions she created lasted long after her death.

Augustina de León Alderete, the great-granddaughter of Doña Patricia de la Garza de León (1777–1849) and Don Martín de León, the founders of Victoria, is shown with her husband.

Doña Maria del Carmen Calvillo (1765–1856) of Floresville was one of Texas's earliest ranchers.

More than sixty Spanish or Mexican land grants were awarded directly to women. Others inherited land grants from their husbands or fathers. Some of these women controlled vast areas of land and wealth.

Doña María del Carmen Calvillo

Doña María del Carmen Calvillo scandalized her neighbors by riding a large white stallion around the ranch to supervise her crews, with her long black hair flying in the wind. She rode, dressed, shot, and roped as well as a man.

In 1814, Doña María inherited El Rancho de las Cabras (the Ranch of the Goats) from her father. It was near the Paso de las Mujeres (Crossing of the Women) in Wilson County. She increased the ranch's livestock to 1500 cattle and 500 goats, sheep, and horses. She built a large irrigation system, a sugar mill, and a granary with the help of a work force of twenty families.

Although her neighbors had trouble with the Native Americans, Doña María was a smart diplomat. Over the years she provided neighboring tribes with cattle and grain, and they never attacked her ranch.

Mrs. Brigadier-General

María Cassiano (1790–1832), a descendant of María Betancour (San Antonio's founder) was another woman of influence. In 1808, she married the Spanish governor of Texas and ran the affairs of state in his absence. She conducted military reviews in front of the Governor's Palace while mounted on her spirited horse. The officers and soldiers called her La Brigadiera (Mrs. Brigadier-General).

Texas's First Cattle Queen

Doña María Hinojosa de Ballí (1760–1801), an influential, powerful woman, was Texas's first cattle queen. She controlled a vast area of ranchland along the Rio Grande. Her home was in Reynosa, Mexico, but her ranch headquarters were at La Fería, Texas.

Doña María inherited her husband's land grants after his death in 1790. She ultimately owned one-third of the present lower Rio Grande Valley including Padre Island, named after her son, a priest. Doña María made her mark on the history of the border, helping lay the groundwork for one of the state's most important industries. Many communities in that region were a direct outgrowth of her ranching enterprise.

Descendants of the Canary Islanders who founded San Antonio lay a wreath at the Spanish Governor's Palace. Maria Betancour (1703–1779) was known as La Pobladora, *(the Foundress).*

"Give us men with families."
— *Order by Spanish authorities
to colonizing expeditions*

María Betancour (1703–1779)

In 1731, forty-five years before the American Revolution, María Betancour, a widow with five children, led thirty-one Canary Islanders to found Texas's first permanent European settlement in San Antonio. María named the main square around which the first buildings were constructed the Plaza de las Islas. The settlement soon bloomed with shade trees, fruitful plants, and colorful flowers. María's home was filled with beautiful furnishings and heirlooms and was the scene of many social gatherings. María later married another settler, Lorenzo de Armas, and they had five more children.

María Betancour's will was filed in the Royal Presidio of San Antonio de Bexar on January 5, 1779. In it she attested to her origins, religious faith, financial status, marriages, and children. The following excerpt includes the major clauses:

Now that I am afflicted with all the infirmities and aches inevitable to old age ... I now name as my advocate and guide the Empress of the Heavens, Holy Mary, my Lady and Mother. I hereby publish the last will and testament of all my property ... one day of irrigation water ... in the Lower Labor ... The suerte ... of land called Del Palmo Quemade ... the stone house in which I live ... all the cattle ... which bear my brand ... a ranch ... on the other side of Cibolo Creek ... one chest which I brought from the Canary Islands, an image of Our Lady of the Immaculate Conception, and four other images of various saints ... To my granddaughter ... I have left the mattress and quilt which I am using. I gave the woolen skirt to Josefa de Seguro. I leave the branding iron to my son Juan.

Some pioneers earned a living selling butter, eggs, and birds in the market.

Most of the women in Texas during the colonial period and for the rest of the nineteenth century were not wealthy like Doña María Hinojosa de Ballí, or influential like María Betancour. They led ordinary lives of hard work. They were wives, mothers, farmers, shepherdesses, small ranchers, midwives, laundresses, seamstresses, cooks, peddlers, and potters. They were poor and remain anonymous, and their history remains to be written.

The work and contributions of Hispanic women have been crucial to the development of Texas and the preservation of community values. While the Amerindian culture is the oldest, the Hispanic one is the oldest continuous culture in Texas.

María Josefa Granados owned the largest general store in San Fernando (San Antonio) in 1787. It carried everything from a pin to a saddle, a diaper to a party dress, even a chamber pot without a handle. Most people in town owed her money, and her list of debtors is a good census of her community for that year. Another pillar of the San Antonio community was María Josefa Becerra Seguín, an early San Antonio landowner, who wrote to her husband describing the steps she had taken to secure her water rights from the city.

A BEAUTIFUL FIGURE ... WITH THE ENERGIES OF MASCULINE VIGOUR.
—J. C. Clopper, 1828

Jane and Kian Long

Jane Long was one of the first Anglo settlers in Texas. Her slave Kian was a lifetime companion. They arrived in 1819, following Jane's husband Dr. James Long, an adventurer who wanted to end Spanish rule of Texas. In 1820, Long headed for battles in Mexico, leaving Jane and Kian on deserted Bolivar Island across from Galveston. The two women survived a brutal winter, and Jane gave birth in an ice-covered tent. She is sometimes called the Mother of Texas.

After Dr. Long was killed in Mexico, Jane and Kian returned to Mississippi and reentered Texas as part of Stephen F. Austin's Old Three Hundred in 1824. In 1834, Jane and Kian opened an inn in Brazoria on a well-traveled route. On September 8, 1835, Stephen F. Austin addressed 1000 men at the inn, calling for war against Mexico. For the elaborate dinner and ball that followed, Jane charged seven dollars each, ladies included. Jane maintained close contacts with the leaders of the Texas Republic, and the first gunpowder of the Revolution was stored behind her inn. Inns run by women like Jane Long, Angelina Eberly, and Pamelia Mann gave them access to the affairs of men that they would later lose to the saloons and business offices.

In 1837, Jane and Kian opened another inn on a Richmond land grant. It later became Mirabeau B. Lamar's headquarters during his campaign for the Republic's presidency. She then moved to a nearby plantation which prospered. By 1850 it was one of sixteen in Texas worth more than $10,000. An ardent Confederate supporter, Jane spent her last years rocking on her front porch and smoking her pipe.

Jane Long (1798–1880) was one of Texas's first Anglo settlers.

The great-granddaughters of Kian Long, who was Jane Long's slave and lifelong companion.

The Old Three Hundred

Stephen F. Austin opened the door to widespread North American and slave immigration to Texas in the 1820s after receiving approval from the Mexican government to settle colonies. His Old Three Hundred settlers included a number of women like Elizabeth Tomlinson, who received a land grant as a widow. Another widow, Therese Jurgens, appeared in 1838 before the Board of Land Commissioners of Austin County as administrator of her husband's estate and claimed a league and labor as his headright.

15

Mary Crownover Rabb (1805–1882), pictured with her husband John Rabb, described her pioneer experiences in Travel and Adventures in Texas in the 1820s.

...thar was no hous thar then nore nothing but a wilderness not eaven a tree to cut down to marke this plais.

— Mary Crownover Rabb

Mary Crownover Rabb

Mary Crownover Rabb personifies the experience of many Anglo pioneer women. A Methodist from Arkansas, she came to Texas as a bride in 1822. Her husband John built Texas's first sawmill. The couple gave the lumber for San Antonio's first Methodist church and helped found the first Methodist college in Texas — Rutersville — in 1840 near La Grange. It had a female department. Mary was a member of the Foreign Missionary Society, to which she and John contributed 1100 acres.

Mary was the mother of nine children. An infant son died after exposure during the Runaway Scrape, as the Rabbs fled with other families before Santa Anna's army. Her husband fought at San Jacinto, one son during the Mexican War, and two others fought for the Confederacy. She lived through sixty years of turbulence, warfare, and government changes.

Immigrant Women

Anglo women of all social and economic classes came to Texas during the nineteenth century. They came as newlyweds or with their families; sometimes they came alone as widows or single women. They came from the Deep South, trans-Appalachia, Europe, and New England. They came overland in wagons and on ships. Some brought their slaves; most had none. They lived in towns, on small farms, or on plantations. In the beginning, they settled along the Gulf Coast and in East and Central Texas.

Few of the women who came to Texas as settlers were ill-prepared for life on the frontier. Many came from farms and had experiences on other frontiers. Because their husbands were often away for long periods of time, women ran ranches and farms for months at a time.

Women worked alongside their husbands, children, and in many cases slaves, to survive. The weather was severe (blue northers were legend), and illnesses and epidemics took their toll. Nevertheless, women worked from the beginning to establish a community life and perpetuate values remembered from their home communities.

Women on the frontier were scarce. In some of the colonies, there were twice as many men as women. The labor and companionship of women were highly valued, and all women who wished to do so, easily found husbands.

Mary Austin Holley's Advice to Women Contemplating a Move to Texas:

Housekeepers should bring with them all indispensable articles for household use, together with as much common clothing (other clothing is not wanted) for themselves and their children as they conveniently can. Ladies in particular should remember that, in a new country, they cannot get things made at any moment, as in the old one.

Those who must have a feather bed had better bring it, for it would take too long to make one. ... Everybody should bring pillows and bed linen. Mattresses ... are made of moss, which hangs on every tree. They cost nothing but the case and the trouble of preparing the moss. The case should be brought. Domestic checks are best, being cheap and light, and are sufficiently strong. The moss is prepared by burying it in the earth until it is partially rotted. It is then washed very clean, dried and picked; when it is fit for use ... Those who like a warmer bed in winter can put some layers of wool, well carded, upon the moss, taking care to *keep this side up*.

Mary Austin Holley (1784–1846) wrote Texas, Observations Historical, Geographical, and Descriptive, *in 1833.*

The colony will ... ultimately flourish. ... Texas is ... the most eligible part of North America
— Mary Austin Holley, *Texas*, 1833

Mary Austin Holley, a Connecticut widow, wrote *Texas, Observations Historical, Geographical and Descriptive.* The bright and witty book was widely circulated and stimulated emigration from other states to Texas. It was so popular she expanded it into a longer version with guide materials, a defense of the Texas Revolution, and an encouragement to prospective settlers to make Texas their home.

Holley speculated in Texas land, hoping population growth and rising values would help pay off her debts and provide her and her son with financial security. Her profits came to little; she died a governess in Louisiana.

In the 1833 version, Holley praised Texas in glowing terms, and compared it to Eden:

... no state on the continent is more eminently favored by nature, in fertility of soil and salubrity of climate than Texas, or presents a like combination of natural advantages.

... A genuine Yankee could luxuriate here in a paradise of pumpkins ... some of them weighing from four to seven pounds ...

... The displays of vegetable nature in Texas are profuse, various, and valuable; presenting, on one hand, the stately and magnificent forest, and again delighting the eye with the rich and splendid scene of the luxuriant prairie, garnished with an endless variety of beautiful and fragrant flowers; making a landscape of indescribable and surpassing loveliness. It would be an elysium for the florist and the poet. One feels, amid such scenes, as we suppose Adam to have felt when ... he was made the first and sole tenant of Eden ...

I spent the day melting lead in a pot, dipping it up with a spoon, and moulding bullets.
— Dilue Rose Harris

Dilue Rose Harris

Dilue Rose Harris came to Texas with her family in 1833 from St. Louis. She remembered that "There was no church nor preacher, school house nor court house in use." Married when not yet fourteen, she was widowed at forty-four, raised nine children, and lived to be eighty-nine. Her home in Richmond, Texas, still stands.

Dilue and her family were among the refugees caught up in the "horrors of the Runaway Scrape." Her *Reminiscences* are the fullest account of that episode. The Runaway Scrape was the flight of Texans from their homes toward Louisiana in advance of General Santa Anna's troops before the battle of San Jacinto. There was great confusion and panic, and the refugees suffered terribly.

Dilue Harris wrote,

> The horrors of crossing the Trinity are beyond my power to describe. One of my little sisters was sick. ... Mother was not able to travel; she had nursed an infant and the sick child until she was compelled to rest . . . we had buried our dear little sister at Liberty.

The family camped on the San Jacinto battlefield five days after Sam Houston's victory.

The Reminiscences *of pioneer Dilue Rose Harris (1825–1914) are an important source of early Texas history.*

She Was a Mann After All

Next to Sam Houston, Pamelia Mann was the most talked about person in the Texas Republic. During the Runaway Scrape, Pamelia loaned Houston her oxen to pull his cannon, but only on the condition he head toward Nacogdoches. When Houston ordered the wagon turned in the opposite direction, Mrs. Mann overtook the army, wearing a pair of pistols and carrying a long knife on her saddle. She accused Houston of lying, cussed him, and demanded the return of her oxen. Houston replied, "Madam, don't irritate me." Mann retorted, "Irritate the devil. I am going to have my oxen." She drew her pistol, rode up beside the driver, and told the oxen to *whoa*. She then cut them loose and drove them away.

The Runaway Scrape

One wife tried unsuccessfully to get her cowardly husband to defend their family during the Runaway Scrape. When he refused, she said, "Well, I will. If I can get a gun, I'll be durned if I don't go behind that breastwork and fight with those men." She got an old musket and remained half the night defending the settlement.

Suzanna Wilkinson Dickinson

In 1836, with the Mexican Army approaching, Suzanna Dickinson's husband took her and their baby to the Alamo for safety. While there, she cooked, nursed, and tried to boost morale. Her husband died during the siege, along with the other men. After the defeat of the Texans, Santa Anna gave Suzanna an escort to Gonzales where she brought the news to Sam Houston. She later received a generous land grant from the Republic of Texas.

Madame Andrea Candelaria

Madame Andrea Candelaria, one of the few Mexican women inside the Alamo during its siege, nursed James Bowie. Almost fifty years after the battle, the Texas Legislature granted her a pension as an Alamo survivor and for nursing services she rendered during smallpox epidemics in San Antonio. She died at the age of 113.

Suzanna A. Dickenson (1820–1883) was one of the survivors of the Alamo.

How Women Won the Second Battle of the Alamo

Although the Texans lost the first battle of the Alamo in 1836, the women won a second battle seventy-five years later. In 1903 Adina De Zavala of San Antonio organized a chapter of the Daughters of the Republic of Texas to save the Alamo from commercial exploitation. When their fund raiser ran aground, a young woman named Clara Driscoll wrote checks for $25,000 — her first act of philanthropy, but far from her last — to buy the adjacent land. The Texas Legislature later reimbursed Clara Driscoll, and the Alamo was turned over to the DRT to maintain as a historical shrine.

Madame Andrea Castanon Candelaria (1785–1899), a Mexican woman, nursed Jim Bowie in the Alamo and was awarded a state pension of twelve dollars a month.

The Yellow Rose of Texas — Emily [D. West] Morgan

The Battle of San Jacinto was the last military event of the Texas Revolution. On March 13, 1836, General Sam Houston and his army defeated the Mexican general Santa Anna in eighteen minutes. Some historians have praised Houston's military accomplishment. Others have attributed a part of Houston's success to vital assistance by a mulatto named Emily Morgan. (It is not known if she was a slave, an indentured servant, or free.)

Emily Morgan caught Santa Anna's eye as he passed a coastal plantation and was taken by him to the San Jacinto battlefield. Emily supposedly sent word to Sam Houston, alerting him to Santa Anna's route. Legend has it that she "distracted" Santa Anna prior to Houston's attack, resulting in the

Mexican Army being unprepared. Hence, Houston's eighteen-minute victory.

After the Texans won the Battle of San Jacinto, Emily Morgan was rewarded for her patriotism with her freedom and a passport back to her New York home. She was immortalized in the song "The Yellow Rose of Texas."

Wars and revolutions marked much of nineteenth century life in Texas. Women of all ethnic groups were active participants in the Texas War for Independence, the Mexican War, the Civil War, and the battles between Native Americans, North American, European, and Spanish settlers over possession of the land. Women were cooks, nurses, soldaderas, warriors, propagandists, camp followers, laundresses, and suppliers of food, clothing, and medicine.

Señora Francisca Alvarez, like so many women before and after her, took pity in 1836 on captured prisoners of war. The wife of a Mexican Army officer, she was called the Angel of Goliad for saving the lives of Texans imprisoned after that battle.

Angelina Eberly (1804–1860) fired a cannon in downtown Austin in 1842 to prevent Sam Houston's men from moving the state's archives to Washington-on-the-Brazos. Her actions helped keep Austin the state capital and her inn filled with customers.

The Mexican War (1846–1848)

The annexation of Texas by the United States precipitated a war with Mexico. Sarah Borginnis, "The Great Western," traveled with General Zachary Taylor's army. A giant of a woman six feet tall, she cooked, washed, loaded cartridges, and dressed wounds. She was awarded a medal posthumously. Many other women on both sides of the border performed similar duties.

Teresa Viele, the wife of a U. S. Army officer in Rio Grande City, recalled: "The well known devotion of the Mexican women to the sick and wounded of our army ... finds no parallel."

After the war ended, there were skirmishes and armed battles in South Texas for the rest of the nineteenth century. Mexican and border Hispanic women were part of this resistance movement that continued to claim that area as part of Mexico.

Jane (McManus) Cazneau (1807–1878)

Writer Jane Cazneau was the only woman awarded an empresario grant to develop land in Texas. She had earlier championed Texas annexation through fiery articles in Eastern papers. Cazneau was instrumental in developing a secret peace mission to Mexico City in 1846, accompanying her *New York Sun* publisher. Fluent in Spanish, she was the first war correspondent to report from behind the battle lines.

Although she favored annexation of Northern Mexico and a canal through that country, she condemned the military of both the U. S. and Mexico. She branded Santa Anna and his generals as tyrants who oppressed that country's working classes. She also criticized the U. S. Navy for hanging a sailor as punishment for insulting an officer, while an American army unit which plundered a Mexican village went unpunished. Under the pen name of Cora Montgomery, she wrote *Eagle Pass* in 1852.

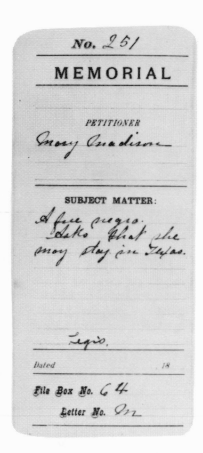

Free women of color were among the first Texas women to take political action.

Free Women of Color

Free women of color were Texas pioneers. There were a number of blacks, both free and slave, in Spanish Texas. In 1792, the Spanish census listed 186 mulattos and Negro women as free citizens. Others came to Texas after Mexico outlawed slavery in 1830. They were nurses, laundresses, and domestics. At least three of the early settlers in Stephen F. Austin's colonies were free blacks.

When the Republic of Texas banned free blacks in 1840, a number of free people of color petitioned the Texas Congress (and later the legislature after Texas joined the Union) for the right to remain as free citizens. Mary Madison, a nurse, and Zilpha Husk, a washerwoman, were both free women of color and among the first Texas women to take political action.

Mary Madison had come to Galveston around 1841. Her petition, submitted around 1849, was signed by eighty white Galvestonians who attested to her kind and tender care of the sick and praised her as a valuable citizen. Her petition was granted around 1850.

Zilpha Husk arrived in Houston with her daughter Emily in 1835, "a good and industrious woman peaceably earning her own livelihood." Her 1839 petition to the Texas Congress was denied, but she stayed anyway. Fanny McFarland, another Houston laundress and free woman of color, also petitioned but was denied. She, like Zilpha Husk, defied the authorities and stayed in Harris County until 1866, where she engaged in real estate transfers and made a nice profit.

Although most free people of color were townspeople, a few like Harriet Reynolds, a widow and rancher, lived in the country. She owned $3,300 in cattle, according to the 1860 census of Jackson County.

The state of Texas was shaped by the hands of women — many of them black women. Whose hands planted the seeds which grew into a prosperous Texas agricultural economy?

    — Myra McDaniel, Texas Secretary of State, 1985

Black women were sold on the island of Galveston as early as 1818. Others were pioneers who arrived with Stephen F. Austin's Old Three Hundred in the 1820s. They came chained in ships and overland in wagons, and they came on foot; and some were roped together. Importation of slaves to Texas continued until the end of the Civil War.

Slavery was a profitable institution for some owners, but devastating for many women. Working under the threat of physical punishment or death, and without pay, most slave women were field hands. They cleared land, chopped cotton, cut wood, and built fences. Some, like Caroline of the Peach Point Plantation near Hempstead, could pick 345 pounds of cotton a day. Women shelled corn, killed hogs, built roads, and dug wells. Many had responsibilities as house slaves as well as field work. House slaves cooked, cleaned, washed, ironed, spun, sewed, and wove cloth. They cared for white children as well as their own; they were wet nurses and midwives. In addition, they were expected to bear children to increase their owners' wealth. Rapes and attempts at forced breeding were common. Despite these conditions, slave women resisted their treatment by refusing to be whipped, running away, and sometimes killing their owners.

On the eve of the Civil War, one of every four Texans was a slave — about 180,000 men, women, and children. Most lived on plantations and farms in Central or East Texas. The economic value of a slave child increased $100 each year until he or she was worth top price of about $1,200 as a teenager.

Women were slave owners as well as slaves. The 1860 census listed two women (of the fifty-one planters) who owned 100 or more slaves. They were Mrs. Rebecca Hagerty, a Creek Indian woman of Marion County, who owned 102, and Grace M. Byrd of Polk County, with 105. Hagerty, forty-five, came from Georgia and had real property of $35,000 and personal property of $85,000. Byrd, forty-seven, also from Georgia, had $30,000 in real property and $150,000 in personal property.

The labor of female slaves was essential to the development of the Texas agricultural industry.

SOME SLAVES WERE SOLD LIKE MULES, "TREATED HORRID," AND RESISTED

At the same time, I will sell for each in hand, two negro women, a fine Rockaway carriage, and two harness mules.
— Wm. P. Milby, Indianola, August 23, 1853

"Mother Was Treated Horrid"

"I remember seeing my mother beat all over the head and back one day as she was sweeping the floor, because she asked her mistress to let her go see my little sick brother. ... [He] lay there in the cabin all day long deathly sick until he died. ... Mother was not allowed to go to the grave, but was sent to the creek to wash."
— Interview with a Travis County ex-slave

Louisa Picquet Buys Her Mother's Freedom

In 1860 an ex-slave, Louisa Picquet, raised $1,000 in Ohio to purchase her mother, Elizabeth Ramsey, a Matagorda slave, after a twenty-year search. They had been sold away from each other in 1839. Louisa took an ad in the *Cincinnati Daily Gazette*, October 15, 1860, to thank the donors.

Resistance of Slave Women

Subjected to frequent violence and the splitting of families, slave women resisted the institution both openly and covertly. They broke tools, ran away, and sometimes murdered their masters.

Pregnant Rachel and her five children, ages two to twelve, escaped into Indian territory. Emily, the slave of Thomas Gardner, ran away in January, 1845. An ad in the *Houston Telegraph and Texas Register* noted, "the only article carried off ... is a dark colored, coarse blanket." The sheriff of Sabine County ran an ad in the *Journal and Advertiser* of February 21, 1841, asking for apprehension of two Negro women, Nancy and Isabella, who "broke from my custody ... where they were confined for the alledged [*sic*] murder of their master. They are mother and daughter, both black, and the youngest about eighteen years of age." Adolphus Sterne reported in his diary in 1841: "the whole family of Hyde's got Poisoned ... by having the seeds of Jameson weed trown [*sic*] into Coffee, supposed to be done by the negro woman Frances." A Dallas slave, Jane Elkins, was legally hanged in 1853 for having murdered her master. In Fannin County three slaves, including a woman, Emma, were hanged for killing their masters, according to the *Matagorda Gazette* of January 4, 1860.

"A LIKELY MULATTO WOMAN AGED about 23 or 24 years with her two children ... is offered for sale, and a female field hand will be taken in part payment."
— *H. A. Cobb*, Galveston Civilian and Gazette, *August 17, 1848.*

Adeline Waldon was one of hundreds of ex-slaves interviewed by WPA workers during the 1930s. The "Texas Slave Narratives" are at the Barker Texas History Center, UT-Austin.

An Overseer Named Minerva

Some slave women were overseers. John Thomas, a Brazoria planter, described one of his valuable slaves, Minerva, around 1833, "I have a woman called Minerva who I raised from a child. She is a smart field hand and in cotton picking time she picks 300 pounds a day. In my absence she is my overseer, and though she is sometimes saucy she knows better than to give my wife any insolence."

1858

Feb 18—Charles and Emaline hauling cotton
Feb 19—Sarah and Sophia covering with harrows, Patsey and three chaps dropping corn
Feb 22 — Charles and Emaline hauling manure and cotton seed
Mar 3 — Amos, Peggy and Caroline covering corn in new ground wih harrows
Mar 10—Emaline nursing the sick
June 2 — Patsey and Jane working potato patch ... Rachel carrying to the plow hands
June 7—Alsey spinning at the house
June 8 — Patsey and Jane working in overseer's garden
Aug 6—Emaline and Malinda sewing

1859

Jan 1 — Lewis and two women hauling rails [for Southern Pacific] ... Patsey spinning fine thread
Jan 5—Three women attending to the lard
Mar 8—Charles and Elsa hauling rails
June 1—Harriett ... nursing Mrs. Webster's baby
June 4—Synthia and Patsey working potatoes
Aug 1—Patsey cooking ... Emaline peeling peaches
　　　　—Excerpts from the Plantation Journal of John B. Webster, Harrison County

If they ever caught them a-praying, they'd get a whipping.
　　　　—Rosie Williams

"I Cheated Maser"

Owners increased their wealth by encouraging slaves to bear children. Some owners even forced their slaves to breed. But Mary Gaffney defeated the ambition of her master to "raise him a lot more slaves ... I cheated Maser. I never did have any slaves. ... I kept cotton roots and chewed them all the time [believed to accomplish birth control] but I was careful not to let Maser know or catch me. Yes, after freedom we had five children."

Some irons used by slaves had bells in the handles. When the bells stopped ringing, the mistresses knew the slaves had stopped ironing.

Grandmother remembered very well the day they sold her mother.
— Annie Mae Hunt

Slave families were often split apart through sales to different purchasers. Or sometimes when an owner died, he left various members of a slave family to different heirs in his will. Separations of children from their mothers, husbands from their wives, and brothers from their sisters were remembered with great sadness by ex-slaves in the "Texas Slave Narratives" and other reminiscences.

Annie Mae Hunt, in her oral history, *I Am Annie Mae,* recalls the sale of a family member:

> My grandmother's name was Matilda, Matilda Boozie . . . My grandmother was known as a house girl. That means you worked in the house with Old Mistress . . . My grandmother always said she remembered very well the day they sold her mother. I don't know how old she was, but she was able to work, she was in the house with Old Mistress. And grandmother cried and cried, and Old Mistress hugged her and told her, 'Don't worry, Tildy. I'll take care of you.' And she did. She took care of her. 'Don't worry, Tildy. I'll take care of you.' That's all Grandma knew. She had sisters and a brother, and she never heard from them no more.
>
> When I got to be a grown woman and had all these children, there was a lady down in Fayetteville, Texas, near where we were, who had the same name that Grandma had, come from the same place — South Carolina. It was my boyfriend's grandmother. And my grandmother and his grandmother looked just alike. But by them being old, it was hard for Grandma to go see about her. She always said, 'I'm going down and talk to Mrs. Dobb's mother.' But she never did.

Matilda Boozie Randon, an ex-slave and midwife, with her husband, the Reverend Eli Randon, a Washington County preacher, holding their grandson George.

Matilda Boozie Randon

Matilda Boozie Randon and her husband had 1500 acres of land that had been given to them after the Civil War by her former owner because she had borne a child to the "young mawster." They were successful farmers, and other black families worked for them as laborers and sharecroppers. They also sold foodstuffs to their employees after the "company store" model.

2

CIVIL WAR AND EARLY COMMUNITY BUILDING

During Texas independence and early statehood, the Native Americans were pushed out of most of East and Central Texas, and Mexicans experienced a new wave of racism. Doña Patricia de León, for instance, a widow who had supported Texas independence, was forced to leave the state, and her extensive property was stolen. White immigration, meanwhile, was swelled by emigrants fleeing the revolutions of the 1830s and 1840s in Europe, as well as by pioneers from the United States. Writers like Jane Cazneau and Norwegian Elise Waerenskjold were among the early promoters of Texas immigration. Immigrant women built a religious and cultural life for their new communities in Texas. Some, like Elisabet Ney and Amelia Barr, were artists and writers. Some, like Waerenskjold, distributed cuttings from fruit trees, demanded construction of schools, and even spoke out against slavery.

"I am convinced that in time slavery will be abolished either by gentle means or by force, because I believe that institutions founded on injustice cannot survive, but are doomed to fail," Waerenskjold wrote. Barr described women who opposed Texas secession from the Union. Melinda Rankin, a Presbyterian missionary, was fired from her job for her Union sympathies. And Chipita Rodriguez, an elderly, respected innkeeper in San Patricio, was hanged in 1863 for a murder she did not commit — possibly framed because she gathered information for the Union. Women united across race lines to protest her sentence.

While the men fought the Civil War, white women labored with their slaves to run the planta- tions, and they made clothing and bandages for soldiers, working day and night. The war imposed serious hardships on those at home. Ursuline nuns in Galveston turned their convent school into a hospital. Pro-Confederate heroines included spy Mollie Bailey, gunrunner Sally Scull, and "Paul Revere" Sophia Coffee Porter.

During the Reconstruction period following the Civil War, blacks made phenomenal advances in education and community building. Black women were essential in establishing churches and schools and reuniting families, and they supported black men in the exercise of their new right to vote. Both black and white women were among the teachers who taught in freedmen's schools. Some whites, however, fought against new black educational and political rights and economic liberty with raids, rapes, and lynchings.

The 1870s saw the organization of formal benevolent aid societies among all ethnic and religious groups for nursing the sick and caring for orphans and the elderly, as well as for missionary work and self-improvement. Involvement in such organizations was the beginning of a great change for women — their movement in increasing numbers out of purely domestic spheres and into the public arena. In the years to come, many public institutions we now take for granted would be founded or held together by the efforts of women. Schools, churches, synagogues, libraries, kindergartens, and hospitals were among women's highest civic priorities, along with legal reform, social welfare institutions, the arts, civil rights, sanitation, public health, and beautification.

27

Many women like Sophia Coffee Porter (1815–1897) lost their husbands or relatives during the Civil War.

Brother Joe made us his last visit in 1863. I saw him mount his horse, Grey Eagle, and ride away never to return. Oh, war, cruel, cruel war.
—*Eudora Moore*

Texans were split over the issue of slavery and support for secession and the Confederacy, just like citizens in other states. For the most part, Texas women supported the Confederacy by running farms and plantations, sewing for the soldiers, and keeping up morale. Others agreed with Governor Sam Houston, who opposed secession.

Sally Scull and Sophia Coffee Porter were two women who played active roles in the Confederate war effort. Sally Scull (1816? – 1877) was a successful horse trader who became a gunrunner during the Civil War. She freighted cotton in wagons to the Rio Grande, where she exchanged it for munitions for the Confederacy.

The Civil War found Sophia Porter and her husband running a trading post on the Red River. Once when a group of Yankees were quartered at her home, she gave them the key to the wine cellar. After they were drunk, she got on her mule, forded the icy river, and went to warn Confederate troops of their presence. She was called the Texas Paul Revere.

Elise Waerenskjold (1815–1895) was a pioneer writer and community leader from Norway who opposed slavery.

Elise Waerenskjold

Elise Waerenskjold was a community leader for almost fifty years in Four Mile Prairie, east of Dallas. She settled there in 1847, after a fruitful career in Norway as a woman's leader, teacher, editor, and temperance advocate.

Known as the "walking newspaper," she traveled frequently among Norwegian settlements, where she was treated "like a bishop." She sold magazine subscriptions, started a reading club, and taught school. She favored Texas's homestead laws because they protected property rights of women.

Waerenskjold wrote articles for Norwegian publications about life in Texas, and was the author of numerous letters, published as *Lady with a Pen*. In 1888, she was still subscribing to Norwegian feminist magazines.

"I am convinced that in time slavery will be abolished either by gentle means or by force, because I believe that institutions founded on injustice cannot survive, but are doomed to fail."
— Elise Waerenskjold

"I have heard my mother say many times that slavery was a curse to the South and was wrong in every way, that she was glad they were freed, that the North was on the side of right and that right prevailed."
— Sallie Reynolds Matthews, *Interwoven*

"My husband was a staunch opponent of slavery, and did not hesitate to express his views. . . . I received word that . . . my husband . . . had been hanged from the limb of one tree."
— Claire Feller, Fredericksburg

Not all Texans supported slavery. Some, like Elise Waerenskjold and Melinda Rankin, were vocal in their opposition. Amelia Barr reported in her autobiography that Lucille, a sixteen-year-old Unionist friend of hers, spat from the gallery on the Ordinance of Secession as the lieutenant governor was taking the oath of allegiance to the Confederacy. "There was a little soft laughter from the women sympathizers." Slaves continued to resist the institution. Many ran away — to Mexico or to live with Native Americans. Rumors of slave revolts spread during this period.

Elise Waerenskjold considered slavery an "abomination" contrary to the will of God: "I believe to the fullest degree that human beings are born with equal rights." When asked by neighbors if she would accept a Negro woman as a daughter-in-law, she responded that it would not please her very much, but "I would rather have it thus than to have grandchildren who are slaves."

Melinda Rankin, a Presbyterian missionary, was fired from her job as director of the Rio Grande Female Seminary in Brownsville for Abolitionist sympathies (see page 46).

Sarah Archer was a pioneer Texan. Spinning thread and weaving cloth were very time-consuming.

Harriet Person Perry of Marshall recorded in a daybook and letters to her husband how the white women and the slaves stayed up late into the night making cloth and sewing for the soldiers. "Mrs. Murrah is so busy, she makes her negroes spin until 10 or 12 o'clock at night. Your mother is making 90 yards of cloth a week — two looms going all the time." In Austin, the Ladies Needle Battalion met at the Capitol and sewed for the soldiers.

Shortages of food and clothing plagued those at home. Basic items were in short supply, and prices were high. Some women dug up the floors of their smokehouses and leached the salt drippings. In 1864, Galveston women gathered at the quarters of the Confederate island commander, protesting shortages and demanding rations of flour and bacon instead of the cornmeal being sold at inflated prices. Their ringleaders were placed under guard, interrogated singly, and then ordered off the island.

Aunt Mariah Carr, an ex-slave, remembered: "I spun thread to make clothes for the Confederate soldiers."

Lizzie Scott Neblett (1833–1917) of Grimes County ran the family plantation while her husband was away fighting during the Civil War.

An anonymous slave woman, Colorado County, ca 1852.

The Civil War separated husbands and wives. Jenny and her cousin Lizzie Scott Neblett both had husbands away at the battlefields. Their letters reflect the feelings of wives left behind.

> My husband is up on the eve of leaving me and his babies for the war to set himself up as a target for the abominable Yankees . . . to shoot at . . . never to return I fear. Poor dear fellow. . . . He has said fifty times in the last week, 'if I could leave you provided for I WOULD GO WITH A LIGHT HEART.' I do all I can, and have made two dollars every week, now for 5 or 6 weeks.
>
> The aid society are having clothes made for the soldiers, but will not allow the women more than two dollars worth . . . a week so that all may get a part. That however will not last long. There is very little work going now.
>
> —Jenny to Lizzie Scott Neblett, March 23, 1862

"My heart and love is pinned to your breast."

The husbands of some slaves accompanied their masters to the battles. Once out of Texas, some ran away and joined the Union forces. Harrison County slave Fanny Norflet wrote to her husband:

> My Dear husband, I would be mighty glad to see you and I wish you would write back here and let me know how you're getting on. I am doing tolerable well. . . . I haven't forgot you nor, I never will forget you as long as the world stands even if you forget me. My love is just as great as the first night I married you and I hope it will be so with you. My heart and love is pinned to your breast, and I hope yours is to mine. . . . 'If you love me like I love you no knife can cut our love into.'
>
> — Your loving wife, Fanny [Norflet], December 28, 1862

After the Civil War, black Texans worked hard to establish schools for themselves and their children.

Black women were essential in establishing new communities of freed slaves during the Reconstruction period after the Civil War. They helped build black churches by organizing congregations, raising money, and teaching Sunday School. They reorganized family life and searched for relatives who had been sold away during slavery.

Black Texans organized private schools for themselves and their children as soon as they could. Parents sacrificed to pay the twenty-five- and fifty-cent tuitions. At first these schools were taught primarily by blacks who had managed to acquire reading and writing skills. According to the Freedmen's Bureau state superintendent, they "are desirous of imparting to others what they themselves have learned. These native elementary teachers are of great use, for they are content with a scanty support and penetrate the country where white teachers cannot go."

Women who had been slaves now became members of the paid work force. Their principal occupations were as agricultural laborers (including sharecroppers), farmers, domestics, and laundresses.

The 1880 *Dallas City Directory* listed two black women running their own businesses — a restaurant and a laundry. Others were teachers and seamstresses.

Sharecropping arrangements with black women were not unusual. Ex-slave Dolly Lang entered into a sharecropping contract with Mrs. V. C. Billingsley in 1889 for the use of forty-eight acres and paid her the first three 500-pound bales of cotton as rent.

"We Will Starve No Longer."

In 1877, black laundresses in Galveston went on strike for wages of at least a dollar–fifty a day. This is the first recorded strike of Texas women. They marched through town shutting down steam and hand laundries by driving off workers with threats, and nailed shut the doors and windows of one laundry. The strike followed on the heels of a black stevedores' strike, in which the men went out for two dollars a day. The women's motto was: "We will starve no longer." (*Galveston Daily News*, August 1, 1877)

THE FREEDMAN'S

SPELLING-BOOK.

PUBLISHED BY THE

AMERICAN TRACT SOCIETY,

NO. 28 CORNHILL, BOSTON.

The U. S. Freedmen's Bureau also established schools and furnished teachers and books for Texas's ex-slaves. Men, women, and children all attended. In 1867, there were 1,627 female and 1,348 male students. In 1868, there were nineteen white teachers and thirteen black teachers. Many German Texans supported these efforts and furnished teachers room and board.

Teachers were both male and female, white and black, local and Northern. One Polk County teacher was a poor white woman with seven fatherless children. Both white and black teachers were subjected to harassment and violence. A white Georgetown teacher was expelled from her boardinghouse and received insulting letters. A "colored lady teacher" in nearby Circleville was also compelled to leave the area and return home. During the 1870s the Freedmen's Bureau schools were absorbed into the public school system.

After the Civil War, stray cattle were available for the rounding up. Some women ran crews of roughneck cowboys or roped their own cattle. A few powerful women made decisions involving high finance in the heyday of the cattle industry. Lizzie Johnson was one of the first women to ride the Chisholm Trail to St. Louis. She preferred the company of cowboys to that of bankers. But when she reached the end of the trail, she dressed up and played the part of a rich lady.

Lizzie's mother taught piano and was the neighborhood doctor. Her father founded Johnson Institute in Hays County where Lizzie taught school. Good at figures, Lizzie began keeping books for local cattlemen. Lizzie recognized a good business opportunity and decided to go into the cattle business. She registered her brand in 1871. She parlayed her earnings from bookkeeping and from articles she wrote for *Frank Leslie's Illustrated Weekly* into cattle investments.

Lizzie married a preacher, Hezekiah Williams; an innovator in private life, she insisted they keep their property separate. He was less successful that she, sometimes borrowing money from her which she insisted he repay. They had a friendly rivalry —branding each other's strays.

Lizzie Johnson (1843–1924), one of Texas's most successful cattle dealers, and her husband, the Reverend Hezekiah Williams.

Lizzie believed in diversifying her assets. She secretly bought up a lot of Austin real estate, and after becoming widowed, she lived above a store in downtown Austin. She became very miserly in later life, nearly starving herself to death until a relative arranged for a nearby restaurant to send up a daily bowl of soup. At the time of her death, Lizzie owned property in five counties, leaving an estate of $200,000. Diamonds were found hidden all around her apartment.

Henrietta King (1832–1925) ran the world's largest and most famous ranch for forty years in Kingsville.

Henrietta King ran the world's largest and most famous ranch for forty years from 1885 to 1925.

As a young woman, she taught at the Rio Grande Female Institute in 1854, the year it was opened by Presbyterian missionary Melinda Rankin. Henrietta married Captain Richard King, and together they founded the King Ranch on the 15,500-acre Rincon de Santa Gertrudis grant they bought from the widow of Juan Mendiola for $300. After her husband's death in 1885, Henrietta hired her son-in-law, Robert J. Kleberg, Sr., as ranch manager. Working together, they eliminated a $500,000 debt and doubled the size of her holdings to over one million acres.

Mrs. Henrietta King was a community builder. She donated land for the towns of Kingsville and Raymondville, and founded many local businesses. She constructed the First Presbyterian Church of Kingsville and donated land for the South Texas Teachers College (now Texas A&I University), the Mexican American Industrial Institute, and Spohn Sanitarium, among other institutions.

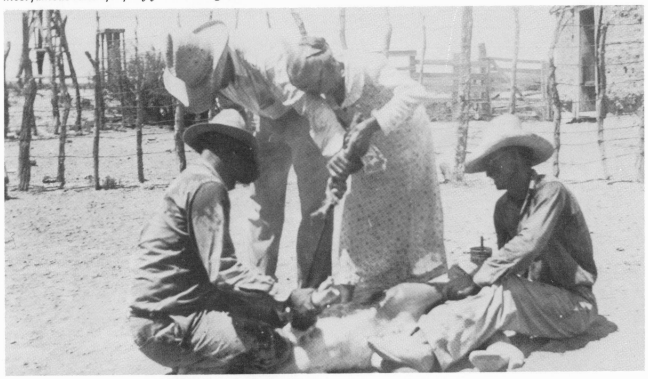

Emma Dehouch (Mrs. Pierre Van) Hollebeke and her three sons brand a calf on their West Texas ranch.

Goat herders at La Mota Ranch, La Salle County, owned by Amanda Burke, 1880s. Some women owned ranches, and some worked on them.

Ellen O'Toole Corrigan (1825–1907) from Ireland ran her San Patricio County ranch with the help of Mexican hands. She and her brother financed the construction of the Sacred Heart of Jesus Church.

Many Texas women like Ellen O'Toole Corrigan and Johanna Wilhelm owned ranches. Mabel Doss Day Lea (1854–1906) of Coleman County was the first Texan to fully fence her ranch. In 1884 she lobbied successfully for a state law making fence-cutting a felony. Later she founded the town of Leaday, settling over 500 families on her land and providing schools and churches. Other women, many Hispanic, worked on ranches as shepherdesses or cooks.

Johanna Wilhelm, the Sheep Queen of West Texas, owned 10,000 sheep in Menard and McCullough counties, more than any other woman in the state, about 1900. Her ranch covered over 100 sections.

Hispanic women have a long tradition of owning ranches. María Hinojosa de Ballí, Doña María del Calvillo, and Doña Patricia de la Garza de León ran ranches in South Texas around 1800 (see pages 10 and 12).

Other Hispanic women like Margarita Villareal (Number 8 below), Florencia Benavides (Number 9 below), and Paula Rodriguez (Number 10), registered their cattle brands (earmarks) in the Nueces County Courthouse in 1867, 1868, and 1869.

Santos Chavarría, Alpine, in the Big Bend, 1901.

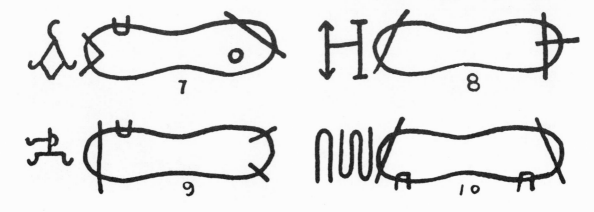

Elisabet Ney (1833–1907) of Muenster, Westphalia, Germany, became famous for her massive sculptures glorifying Texas heroes. Right: Ney created this bronze bust of Sam Houston for the Chicago World's Fair in 1893. Her other statues of Sam Houston and Stephen F. Austin are in the U.S. and Texas Capitol buildings.

Dame nature seems to have had everything here her own way in Texas. . . . The flowers, the insects of every type, and the animals are super-abundant.

—Letters from the Ursuline, 1852–1853
By Irish nuns in San Antonio

Immigrants from Central Europe began coming to Texas in the 1830s, 1840s and 1850s to escape political unrest and poverty. They enriched the state with their families, hard work, ideas, values, and cultural institutions. Among these, the Germans came in large numbers. They were friendly with the Indians and in the main opposed slavery.

Women from France, England, and Ireland also settled in Texas. In Galveston, French sisters of the Ursuline order, a teaching congregation, established a girls' school in 1847. In 1855, Madame Victor Considerant, part of Dallas's French Utopian settlement La Reunion, held a literary salon in a grove of cedars. Toward the end of the nineteenth century, religious repression and economic conditions in Eastern and Southern Europe drove more Europeans to Texas homes.

Louise Heuser Wueste (1806–1874) was a German painter who settled in San Antonio in 1857 and continued her artistic career.

Elisabet Ney

Elisabet Ney was the first of a long line of illustrious Texas women sculptors. Others were Bonnie MacLeary, Allie Tennant, Waldine Tauch, and Electra Waggoner Biggs.

Elisabet Ney knew what she wanted to be at the age of eight — a sculptor. She was ambitious and an intense feminist. At eighteen she went on a hunger strike to force her parents to allow her to study in Munich.

By 1860 she was a renowned European sculptor, doing busts of Garibaldi, "Mad King" Ludwig, and Schopenhauer. Schopenhauer told friends, "If you don't know Sculptress Ney, you have lost a great deal."

Ney married a Scottish physician-philosopher, Dr. Edmund Montgomery, but always kept her maiden name. In 1871, the couple moved to the United States. After two years in Georgia, they bought Liendo Plantation in Hempstead, and Elisabet turned from sculpting to farming and motherhood. She understood little about either. For the next twenty years, she did almost no sculpting.

At the age of fifty-eight, Ney began her "second career." She was invited to Austin by Governor Oran Roberts and obtained a commission to sculpt Texas heroes for the 1893 Chicago World's Fair. In 1891, she set up an Austin studio and home, which became Texas's first museum — the Ney Museum. Her unconventional lifestyle, clothing, and progressive ideas made her a controversial figure. She scorned the traditional female role, saying, "Women are fools . . . to be bothered with housework. Look at me. I sleep in a hammock which requires no making up. I break an egg and sip it raw. I make lemonade in a glass and then rinse it, and my housework is done for the day." Ney entertained the great and the famous — the tenor Caruso, the pianist Paderewski, and the ballerina Pavlova.

An advocate of fine arts education in the public schools, Ney testified before the legislature, pleading for fine arts funding and speaking in favor of suffrage. She was a woman ahead of her time.

Mother Madeleine Chollet (1846–1906) was a French nun and a member of the Sisters of Charity of the Incarnate Word. She and two other sisters founded Santa Rosa Hospital in San Antonio in 1869.

The history of Texas reveals the vital role women have played in the state's development. Women have been the driving force in founding large numbers of schools, libraries, museums, churches, synagogues, symphonies, and hospitals. Often, because what women have done is so much a part of our daily lives, we fail to recognize those accomplishments. The role of women in community-building activities has been for the most part invisible.

Hospitals

The first hospital in Texas was founded by the Sisters of Charity of the Incarnate Word in Galveston in 1866. Women founded hospitals all over Texas. Roman Catholic women's religious orders alone founded forty-one.

Fires, yellow fever, and a strange new climate did not stop a small band of young French Catholic nuns who settled in San Antonio to care for the sick after the Civil War. Led by Mother Madeleine Chollet, the Sisters of Charity of the Incarnate Word founded Santa Rosa Hospital in 1869. St. Paul's Hospital in Dallas was founded in 1898 by the Daugh-

ters of Charity of St. Vincent de Paul. That order also founded Seton Hospital in Austin in 1901, and both Hotel Dieu hospitals in El Paso and Beaumont.

Individual women like May Smith and Clara Driscoll made an impact as well. May Smith's efforts led to the establishment of Dallas's Bradford Memorial Hospital for Babies. Clara Driscoll left her entire estate to set up a children's hospital in Corpus Christi.

Nurse May Smith saved the lives of thousands of malnourished and ill children by setting up a makeshift baby camp on the grounds of Dallas's Parkland Hospital. In 1913, she borrowed Red Cross tents, set up the baby camp, then persuaded doctors and nurses to treat the sick infants she had seen in home visits to charity patients.

By 1929 May Smith persuaded Tom Bradford, Sr., to donate $100,000 for a children's hospital — the forerunner of the Children's Medical Center. When she died in 1938, her obituary read:

> May Smith, mother to 55,000 Dallas babies, trades her nurse's cap for a starry crown in heaven.

Sisters of Charity of the Incarnate Word nurse the sick at one of the nation's largest Catholic medical centers — Santa Rosa Hospital in San Antonio.

There is little work in the world that can surpass that done by organized church women.

— Annie Doom Pickrell

Fannie Breedlove Davis (1833–1915) was the first president of the Texas Baptist Women's Missionary Union and editor of the Texas Baptist Worker *(later* Herald*) from 1889 to 1897.*

Women of all denominations – Protestant, Catholic, and Jewish – played important roles in organizing churches and synagogues and in insuring their survival through fund raising, youth work, and Sunday School teaching. They gained valuable administrative skills and made lasting friendships. Their religious beliefs often led them to tackle major social and community issues. For example, Baptist women raised money for orphanages; Methodist women founded the Young Women's Christian Association; and Jewish women supported kindergartens and literacy programs.

Baptist Women

In 1832, Massie Millard gathered women and children for the first women's prayer meeting in Texas – in the thicket around Nacogdoches. The women prayed for the Mexican and Native American women and for guidance. Annette Lea Bledsoe distributed leaflets and New Testaments, organized other Baptist women, and visited Sunday Schools for twenty-five years. By the time the first church was built, she and Massie Millard had recruited sixty-five women "doing mission work," including making clothes for Native American students.

In 1835, Sister Echols, near Gonzales, refused to hide the *Bible* she was reading from a Mexican justice, although she was breaking the Mexican law that required all settlers to adopt Catholicism.

Dallas's First Baptist Church was organized in 1868 by eight women and three men. By 1872, the church had grown to twenty-five members, mostly women.

Fannie Breedlove Davis

Fannie Davis knew how to organize and raise money, like so many Texas women after her. She was a founder of both the Texas and the Southern Baptist Woman's Missionary Unions in the 1880s. Under her leadership as Texas WMU president, members raised $20,000 for Mexican schools and orphanages and funds to send female missionaries to China and Brazil.

Dear Aunt Fannie:
This is our first letter to you. We are two little saw mill girls. Enclosed please find ten cents for the orphans. I hope that we will have more money to send next time. Mama takes the *Herald*. Lovingly,

Hattie and Georgia Sheffield
— *Texas Baptist Herald*, 1899

After the Civil War, black women organized churches, raised money, and taught Sunday School. Ex-slave Delilah Harris gave the land for the A. M. E. Church in Limestone County. Women developed as administrators and decision makers, and their leadership infused the black women's club movement, the civil rights movement, and many interracial and interfaith efforts.

Dr. Maud A. B. Fuller was one of the great religious and civic leaders of Texas for forty years. She was director and president of the Women's Auxiliary of the National Baptist Convention of America, organizing youth societies, raising funds for missionary work, writing missionary literature, and traveling abroad to establish missions. She founded and edited a newspaper *The Woman's Helper* and wrote *A Guide for Women's Home and Foreign Missionary Societies and Circles*. Dr. Fuller was a delegate to the World Baptist Alliance and flew to Africa many times to further the work of her church.

She assisted her husband in their family business, the Fuller Funeral Home. Although childless, the couple educated fifteen young men and women. Fuller was a schoolteacher, principal, and a volunteer for Guadalupe College in Seguin from 1907 to 1924, touring Texas to raise money for teachers' salaries, equipment, and student scholarships. Her community work in Austin included setting up a home for the aged, visiting prisons, and acting as spokesperson before government agencies. Her work has had a lasting impact upon her state and nation.

Dr. Maud A. B. Fuller of Austin (1890–1971) was a national black Baptist leader for over forty years. Here she addresses a national black Baptist Sunday School Congress in Dallas.

Martha White McWhirter (1827–1904) (first row, seated, third from left) was the leader of the Belton Sanctificationists, a group of women who organized a religious collective around 1870.

Lydia McHenry's letters to the Missionary Board in New York in 1835–1836 were instrumental in sending Martin Ruter to Texas for the expansion of Methodism. She taught in a Washington County girls' boarding school and during the Civil War ran classes in spinning and weaving to furnish clothing for Confederate soldiers.

North Texas women both founded and funded churches. Nancy Cochran donated the land for Dallas's first Methodist church, Cochran Chapel, in 1848. Willie Lewis, in *Between Sun and Sod*, wrote that "The good women of the congregation baked, sewed and gave bazaars in order to raise the initial fund" for a Methodist church in Sherman in 1877.

The first meeting of Texas Methodist women for missionary work was held in Henderson in 1882. In 1894, Mrs. Fannie Heartsill became president of the ninety-three-member Women's Foreign Mission, and they raised $50,000 for a girls' college in Brazil. Mrs. Heartsill wrote, "Come work with me; I will unbar each gate. — /See, China — India — Ethiopia — wait." Many Methodist women became leaders in the temperance, suffrage, and women's club movements.

The Belton Sanctificationists

When Methodist Martha McWhirter created her own religion in 1866 in Belton, many middle-class Central Texas wives followed her, leaving homes and husbands behind. Mrs. McWhirter believed no woman should live with an "unsanctified" or brutal husband, and her beliefs jarred Belton society.

Mrs. McWhirter and her followers wished to escape from economic dependence on their husbands, many of whom were alcoholics and wife abusers. The women pooled their money, sold butter and milk, wove rag carpets, and took in laundry. In the 1870s, they began moving in together and became known as the Belton Sanctificationists.

There were several sensational divorce trials and even a lunacy trial when two brothers from Scotland joined the women's commune. A group of irate husbands took potshots at the McWhirter home, which still stands today with a bullet hole in the front door.

By the 1880s, the group of about fifty women and children (with a few men) had become respected capitalists. They owned three farms, a steam laundry, a hotel, and several rooming houses. They did their own carpentry and dentistry. They donated money to the local railroad spur and opera, and Martha McWhirter was even elected to the local Board of Trade.

In 1899, the group, now nearing retirement age, sold their Belton properties and moved to a large French chateau-type home in Washington, D. C., where they lived quietly and attended meetings of Congress. Around 1901, a capital newspaper ran a full page story about the group headlined "A happy home without husbands." After Mrs. McWhirter's death in 1904, the group gradually diminished, although some members continued to live together for ten more years.

Mrs. C. C. de la Garza prepares the altar in the chapel of the restored Spanish Governor's Palace in San Antonio.

Catholic Women

Hispanic women have been active in Texas Catholic church work as worshipers, educators, nuns, and transmitters of religious values since the 1600s. Catholic women of other ethnic groups have founded schools, hospitals, orphanages, altar societies, and charitable institutions.

Catholic women in San Antonio and other cities have organized a number of fraternal and charitable societies. In 1870, women helped found the St. Joseph's orphanage, and in 1893 the Ladies' Aid Society began at the St. Mary's Roman Catholic Church. In 1917, the Daughters of Isabella and the Carmelite nuns did charity work among the poor.

Home Altars

The creation of home altars has been an important form of religious and artistic expression for Catholic women. The makers are folk artists who use images of the Virgin Mary, Jesus, and the saints; photographs of family members and politicians; and rocks, flowers, and sea shells to express their religious feelings and beliefs.

Jewish Women

Rosanna Osterman (1809–1866) was one of Texas's earliest Jewish leaders. She and her husband settled in Galveston in 1839 and opened a general store. She established the city's first Jewish cemetery, brought the first rabbi to Texas in 1852, and held the first religious services in her home in 1856.

During the Civil War and Union blockade, most Galvestonians left the island. But Rosanna stayed behind to nurse the wounded on both sides and spy for the Confederacy. Her will left funds for charities throughout the nation — hospitals, synagogues, a nondenominational widows' and orphans' home in Galveston, and a hostel for sailors.

Helena Landa and her husband Joseph moved to New Braunfels from England before the Civil War and went into business. After Lincoln's 1863 Emancipation Proclamation, Joseph freed their slaves; he was tried by local Confederates and fled to Mexico to avoid being hanged. Helena operated their general store, flour and sawmills, and cotton gin. She preserved Jewish traditions by reciting Friday night prayers, lighting candles, and observing Passover. Her husband was able to return home after the Civil War.

Helena Landa (1835–1912) of New Braunfels preserved Jewish traditions during the Civil War.

Melinda Rankin, founder of a girls' school in Brownsville, wrote Texas in 1850 *and* Twenty Years of Missionary Labor.

One of the objects to be brought about for the benefit of Texas is the planting of a Female Seminary of high order.
— Melinda Rankin

Melinda Rankin

Melinda Rankin, a Presbyterian missionary, came West to convert the Mexicans. Unable to enter Mexico, she taught first in Huntsville and in 1852, founded the Rio Grande Female Institute for Spanish-speaking girls at Brownsville.

Fired from her post for opposing slavery, Melinda Rankin was forced to leave Texas during the Civil War. She spent the rest of her life teaching black freedwomen in New Orleans and organizing the first Protestant network of schools and missions in Mexico.

God only knows how our husbands can be so indifferent toward a project that is of such great importance to our children. In a society where community spirit is lacking, nothing can thrive and prosper.
— Elise Waerenskjold

Texas's early female academies provided the only quality education available for young women before the public schools were established in the 1870s. Early schools were founded by individuals, religious denominations, or Masonic orders.

Frances Trask (Thompson) (1806–1892) was the first Texas woman to devote herself professionally to teaching. Educated in a New York seminary, she established, in 1834, Texas's first boarding school for girls in Independence.

The Baptists founded Baylor University on the site of Trask's school; Baylor's female department dates from 1851. Andrew Female College, founded in Huntsville in 1852, was the most influential of the Methodist girls' schools. Other early schools founded by women were the Ringwood Seminary in Boston, Texas, Elizabeth Todd, 1844; the Ursuline Academy in Galveston, 1847; and the Live Oak Female Seminary, Rebecca Stuart Red, principal, 1853.

Rebecca Stuart Red moved to Austin, where she founded the Stuart Female Seminary in 1876. It offered a Bachelor of Arts or Science degree, as well as unusual subjects for young women — mathematics, Latin, and natural sciences. She hired excellent instructors and attracted students from all over Texas. The chair of the Seminary's board was Colonel Ashbel Smith, later chair of the first board of regents of The University of Texas.

Lucy Ann Kidd-Key was principal of the North Texas Female College (later Kidd-Key College) in Sherman from 1888 to 1916. It was the best known girls' school in the Southwest. She recruited faculty from Europe and increased the school's enrollment from eighty to 500.

Baylor Female College, Jan. 30, 1898
Dear Mama and Papa: . . . I passed in everything — even in Greek. In Caesar I made 80 . . . for a change today we had turkey and coconut custard. I ate more than I should. . . . Much love to you all from Bertie [Barron].

Educational opportunities for blacks in the nineteenth century were limited. Women of the Northern Presbyterian Church showed their concern by establishing the Mary Allen Seminary (and later Junior College), an industrial school for Negro girls, in Crockett in 1886. Prairie View A&M University began as a normal institute in the 1880s, and young women could obtain a teaching certificate. Most of the founders and contributors of Guadalupe College in 1884 were former slaves. The coeducational school had more females than males and separate industrial departments.

Mattie B. White (18??–1961)

Mrs. Thomas J. (Mattie B.) White, an 1884 graduate of Walden University in Nashville, founded the first and only school for black girls in Austin in 1892.

She was a teacher in the Austin public schools, which were segregated at the time; a State Superintendent of the Mother's Club; and a temperance worker. She taught students at the State Deaf, Dumb, and Blind Institute for Colored Youths in Austin and was an award-winning artist. One of her Texas bluebonnet paintings won first prize at a meeting of the National Women's Federation.

Dolores Burton Linton

Dolores Linton never had children of her own, but she gave her all to children. In 1931, she set up a school for poor black children in Paradise Cove, an isolated black community of San Antonio. The area had no streets, electricity, sewers, churches, or schools. Neighborhood children had to walk twelve miles to attend school.

At the age of twenty-one, in 1931, Linton got permission from the school board to set up a school during the day in a dance hall. She was given a few old desks and textbooks. The first year she had first through seventh grades. As the children grew older, she added grades and taught all of them.

In 1946, the old building was replaced with a Civilian Conservation Corps barracks; the students still had no utilities. Linton was now teaching grades one through twelve during the day and at night earning her Masters of Education degree from Our Lady of the Lake College. In 1952, the barracks were at last replaced with a modern four-room building. She then had four teachers, 150 children, indoor plumbing, and adequate supplies. The school was closed by a civil rights directive in 1966, and Linton moved to a neighboring elementary school.

Dolores Linton's students became nurses, financiers, and business and professional leaders. After her death, she was widely honored, and Our Lady of the Lake named her one of their most distinguished graduates.

Mrs. Thomas J. (Mattie B.) White (18??–1961) was an artist and teacher who established Austin's only private school for black girls in 1892.

Dolores Burton Linton (1910–1971) founded a school in San Antonio for poor children.

Olga Bernstein Kohlberg (1864–1935) led the El Paso Woman's Club to establish the first private kindergarten in Texas in 1892.

Olga Bernstein Kohlberg

Olga Kohlberg brought the idea of preschool training from her native Germany to El Paso. She and the Woman's Club persuaded the local school board to start the first public kindergarten in Texas in 1893, a year after the women had opened a private one. Other women across the state soon took up the kindergarten movement.

Kohlberg led in establishing other community institutions, including El Paso's first public hospital and a sanatorium for babies in New Mexico. She was also a founder of the El Paso Public Library and president of its board for thirty-two years. She devoted her life to civic improvements and the woman's club movement, which she saw as "giving inspiration and enlightenment to those in a community that are organized for special work; civic, humanitarian . . . to set up standards, spread information, and . . . produce leaders."

The Dallas Free Kindergarten

The Dallas Free Kindergarten had an ambitious program. It not only cared for poor children, but also held domestic science classes at three school sites. Handwork, sewing, and cooking classes were available to children and their parents. Like Jane Addams's Hull-House in Chicago, the Neighborhood House was the headquarters for the staff and also the site of the association's oldest kindergarten. Children attending the South Dallas kindergarten played on the land behind the Dallas Cotton Mill. The children were given hot meals, baths, and naps.

The Dallas Free Kindergarten and Industrial Association provided facilities for children of immigrants and cotton mill workers as early as 1903.

Mexican-American teachers started *escuelitas* or "little schools" in Texas around 1911. In some counties Mexican-American children were barred from attending public schools. The *escuelitas*, usually headed by well-educated women from Mexico, offered bilingual education and academic instruction in Mexican history and culture.

Some *escuelitas* had extensive academic programs and public examinations. Others were informal, after-school classes held in the home of a neighborhood teacher. They were often the center of community activity. *Escuelitas* began to decline in the 1950s and 1960s with the movement toward equal public education; and also, the advent of widespread bilingual instruction, still a subject of bitter controversy in the 1980s.

Leonór Villegas de Magnón

Leonór Villegas de Magnón, a native of Mexico City, graduated from Mount Saint Ursula in New York City in 1895 with a diploma in kindergarten teaching. She taught kindergarten in Laredo when she and her husband were separated as a result of the outbreak of the Mexican Revolution in 1910. When the border battles broke out, she transformed her kindergarten into a hospital and nursed the wounded from both sides of the border.

Leonór Villegas de Magnón established a kindergarten in Laredo. When the Mexican Revolution broke out in 1910, she transformed it into a hospital.

Kindergarten students of Leonór Villegas de Magnón, ca. 1910.

Texas has always had its share of "bad women."

Belle Starr (1848–1889), the Bandit Queen of Dallas, dressed like a man, rode with outlaw gangs, and made her living as a dance hall gambler and pianist. She was a Missouri finishing school graduate, but she spent her life defying Dallas society and the law.

A convicted horse thief, Belle was gunned down by an unknown assailant when she was forty-one. Her life story has captivated the American public for one hundred years and has inspired fifty books, a Broadway play, a movie, and several television shows.

Another Dallasite, Bonnie Parker (1910–1934) and her outlaw partner Clyde Barrow and their gang cut a swath throughout the Southwest in the 1930s, robbing banks and terrorizing the countryside. She and Clyde were killed by Texas Rangers and other lawmen in an ambush in 1934. Their career may have looked glamorous, but it ended in disaster. Bonnie predicted their end in a poem she wrote during a stay in jail: "Someday they'll go down together/They'll bury them side by side/To few it'll be grief/To the law a relief — /But it's death for Bonnie and Clyde."

In 1926, Rebecca Bradley, a student at The University of Texas, robbed the Farmer's National Bank of Buda at gunpoint, locked the employees in the bank, and calmly drove back to Austin in her "flivver," where she was promptly arrested.

Prostitution

Prostitution has been present in Texas since the early days when women were scarce. In 1843, the Houston City Council banned "lewd women" from the city limits; the law had little effect. In Old Tascosa, Rowdy Kate, the queen of the Red Light District, presided over Ragtime Anne, Boxcar Jane, and Fickle Flossie.

Mollie Adams was owner of one of Waco's largest and most fashionable houses during that city's era of legalized prostitution in 1890–1915. Prostitutes were required to register monthly, pay a fee, and be examined by a doctor.

In 1908, Reverend J. T. Upchurch, a North Texas minister, wrote a book about prostitution in Dallas, Ft. Worth, and Waco called *Traps for Girls*. He condemned the starvation wages of three- to five-dollars weekly being paid to female workers in stores and factories as responsible for their downfall. He established a home for prostitutes and their children in Waco.

In 1911, prostitution was well advertised in Texas's then-largest city — San Antonio — with the publication of a *Guide to the Red Light District*. By World War I, the Texas Women's Anti-Vice Society, led by suffragist Minnie Fisher Cunningham,

forced municipal leaders to take legal action against prostitutes. After World War I, "Miss Hattie's" in Austin and the "Chicken Ranch" in La Grange, immortalized in the play *The Best Little Whorehouse in Texas*, were well known in Central Texas.

3

"WOMEN'S WORK" AND WOMEN'S EDUCATION

The daily lives of most Texas women today still resemble what they have been historically: long hours of housework and child care. The details, however, have gradually changed. Among other labors, women have gathered food, scraped hides, put up and taken down tepees; ground corn for long hours and scrubbed the laundry in the same position — on their knees; done stoop labor, chopped wood, nursed their own and other people's children; farmed, milked cows, preserved fruits and vegetables, cared for the sick, made company welcome, and kept the outhouse clean. Before the days of factories, women manufactured nearly all the goods that were used in the home as well — like soap, candles, thread, cloth, and clothes.

Long before married women in Texas had the legal right to their own income, women were earning money, too. Some took in boarders; some sold butter and eggs; some did sewing or washing; some taught music; and some did the hardest of manual farm labor alongside their men. Women's work also included nursing and midwifery.

Toward the end of the nineteenth century, women began entering the work force outside the home in larger numbers. Many of their jobs were in traditional roles as waitresses, cooks, and domestic workers; but they also broke new terrain as secretaries, telephone operators, and government clerks. In 1872, Martha Bickler became the state's first female employee as a clerk for the General Land Office.

Women were prominent in the teaching profession even in antebellum days, when teachers in girls' schools were mainly women. In the Texas Republic, female education emphasized moral improvement and refinements leading to marriage. After a hiatus during the Civil War, female academies were reinstituted. Among the founders were Rebecca Stuart Red, Lucy Ann Kidd-Key, and Mattie B. White, who established an academy for black girls.

Texas schools remained racially segregated until integration began to occur in the 1950s, but integration of the sexes started sooner. Waco University, with which Baylor merged in 1886 to form a coeducational school, opened its classes to both sexes in 1865; however, not until 1892 did women receive the same degrees as men. Prior to that, they studied for Maid of Philosophy, Maid of Arts, and Mistress of Polite Literature degrees.

During the last two decades of the nineteenth century, with the development of the public school system, teacher training became important. One third of the 1880 graduates of Sam Houston Normal Institute were women. The University of Texas and Prairie View Normal Institute taught both sexes from their outset in the 1880s. Many Hispanic women were sent to Mexico for their education. In 1895, women teachers outnumbered men for the first time, and teaching began to be seen as a female profession.

Around the close of the century, the new emphasis on practicality and the scientific approach had an impact on women's education. Women began to study and practice new "female professions" — nursing, home economics, social work, and library science — professions viewed as extensions of women's traditional roles. Women in these professions then set up institutions like home demonstration units, visiting nurse programs, and "baby weeks" to improve the skills and conditions of women still at home.

Mary A. Maverick (1818–1898), a pioneer San Antonian, kept a diary for over forty years. It was later published as the Memoirs of Mary A. Maverick.

Marriage and motherhood have been the center of most Texas women's lives. Even those who worked outside the home have had the primary responsibility for housework, child care, nurturing, and the family's social life.

Memoirs of Mary A. Maverick

Mary Maverick was born in Alabama and moved with her family to San Antonio in 1835. During the period of the Mexican War, the family moved to La Grange and later to their Matagorda ranch. They returned to San Antonio in 1847, where Mary lived for the next fifty years. Like so many mothers, Mary Maverick was concerned about children other than her own. In 1888, she chaired a community board of thirteen men and women who organized a home for destitute children.

Maverick kept a diary covering the historic, social, and political events of her day, as well as her personal experiences with children, death, grief, and loneliness. Her published *Memoirs* (1838–1881) are drawn from the diary. Despite the many hard times, there are descriptions of happy times in San Antonio:

> 1841: During this summer, the American ladies led a lazy life of ease. We had plenty of books, including novels, we were all young, healthy and happy and were content with each others'

society. We fell into the fashion of the climate, dined at twelve, then followed a siesta, until three, when we took a cup of coffee and a bath.

> A bathhouse . . . some distance up the river . . . between two trees in a beautiful shade, we went in a crowd each afternoon at about four o'clock and took the children and nurses and a nice lunch . . . Then we had a grand and glorious gossip . . . each one told the news from our far away homes in the 'States,' nor did we omit to review the happenings in San Antonio. We joked and laughed away the time, for we were free from care and happy. In those days there were no envyings, no backbiting.

Loss of Children

Mary Maverick recorded in her diary the death of her seven-year-old daughter Agatha: "Sunday, April 30th, my dear little Agatha took fever. . . . the poor child breathed her last at 2 a.m., Tuesday, May 9th, 1848. Even now, in 1880, after 32 years, I cannot dwell on that terrible bereavement. The child was the perfection of sweetness and beauty . . . her very presence was a flood of sunshine."

Mary Maverick's grief over the loss of five of her ten children was shared by many Texas mothers. Losing a child was a common experience. One out of every ten babies born prior to 1917 died before his or her first birthday.

Freedwomen and their children do the laundry on the McFadden Plantation in Circleville.
Washing and ironing have always been a part of a woman's regular work routine.

Over the years, tools, technology, and times have changed. But housework still remains the primary responsibility of women. Washing, ironing, cooking, cleaning, caring for babies and children — these have been part of women's regular routines since the early days of Texas.

Elizabeth Mathews Carpenter of Plano recorded in her diary entry for December, 1878, a summary of her year's workload:

> I must now count up and see how much work I have done this year or how many articles I have made as is my usual practice. I have done my cooking and other housework about six months in this year and most of that time my washing and ironing with some of the mens help — to work the washing Machine — . . . . During the past year I have made 84 articles — Pieced about 3 quilts — quilted 3 quilts and one comfort — knit and footed about 12 pr of socks and Stocking — attended Sunday School 25 times Social worship and preaching about 30 times — done a great deal of mending and all my housework and cooking washing and ironing six months or about that time — not very many visits except to see the sick but visited them about 30 or more

times so ends my work for the year 1878 — May the Lord bless my labors.

I washed, I cleaned. . . . we are so lonesome.
        — Mrs. Rowland Clyde Burns, 1889 diary

Texans have always valued clean clothes but usually underpaid and gave little credit to those who did the laundry. Laundry has always been the work of women who either did it for their own families or had to hire it done.

The most common paid occupation of nineteenth century Texas women was laundress, and most of these were ex-slaves. In 1877, Galveston laundresses went on strike demanding one dollar and fifty cents a day (see page 32). Two black Dallas laundresses were early entrepreneurs: Hopie Thompson bought downtown property after the Civil War and sold it for $25,000 twenty years later, and Mary McGraw owned her own laundry in 1880.

One West Texas woman got tired of all the work involved in wash day, so she rigged up a dog-powered washing machine. Everything was fine until the poor dog wised up and began running away on Mondays!

Food preparation has always been the most important part of a woman's workday. The kitchen was often the center of family life, and cooking provided a creative outlet, as well as a major responsibility. Cooking, chopping, canning, preserving, and gardening took many hours. But they were essential to a family's good health and survival.

Publishing cookbooks has been a popular way for women's church and synagogue sisterhoods and clubs to raise funds and share their expertise with friends and the broader community. *The First Texas Cook Book; a Thorough Treatise on the Art of Cookery* was published in Houston in 1883 by the First Presbyterian Church Ladies Association. The Texas Woman's University in Denton has one of the world's largest collections of cookbooks.

A cookbook written and published in 1965 by the Temple Emanu-El Sisterhood, Dallas.

A woman grinds corn for tortillas on a metate. *This was back-breaking work.*

A pioneer Texan, Mrs. George Huff, was recorded as a seamstress in the census of 1826. With the growth of Texas towns after the Civil War, women began to get paid for the same domestic chores they had always done — cooking, cleaning, sewing, and doing the laundry. These tasks were needed by newly-arrived men as urbanization developed.

Annie Mae Hunt

Annie Mae Hunt was a single head of household for many years who supported her six children through a variety of jobs and businesses. Many were skills used to operate her own home. She was a domestic but turned her back on that activity to earn her living by sewing, selling Avon, and running a restaurant. She described her work experiences in her oral history, *I Am Annie Mae:*

"When I was raising these first three kids in Dallas during the Depression, after I had left my first husband . . . I had jobs. Like mama, like daughter. I'd wash and iron. Like on Monday morning, I'd get up, I'd go out to Mrs. X's house, wash for her, hang her clothes up. Then I'd go on down to wash for another woman. I've done four washes in one day. . . . I worked for $3.50 a week. . . . I could iron a shirt or a child's dress so a fly couldn't stand on the collar. A fly, he would slip off!

"I had cleaned houses all my life. That's all I knew. Every now and then somebody would pay me 50 cents to make a dress, cause that was a way of life, and that was money."

Mrs. Hunt recalls one day in 1955 when she was waiting for the bus in downtown Dallas, "slippin' and slidin' on ice, shivering," and her conscience began to talk to her. "And it says to me, 'Good as you can sew, good as you can sell Avon . . . you ought to freeze to death.'" So she decided, freezing cold as she was, she was going home. And she told another woman waiting for the bus, "I never intend to clean nobody's house in this town . . . as long as I live." Mrs. Hunt continued with her story:

I come on back home that day, and I called the Avon representative. And the next day I walked up on Bexar Street, and had this man to make me a sign, 'Dressmaking,' to put in my yard, and I went to making dresses and selling Avon. From that day I sold Avon nineteen years . . .

Selling Avon, I went from door to door. No, we didn't have parties, but I'd have coffee a lot of times for the girls and me. I made nice money and would be selling it till yet, but I can't drive, and I can't walk anymore like I used to, and so I had to lay it down . . . When I started selling Avon, we were getting five dollars a week for housework.

I would sell eight or nine hundred dollars worth of Avon in two weeks time. I would only get forty percent of that . . . The average order was three to eight dollars . . .

I tried to send all of my children, that would go, to college . . . you can do so many things with education that you can't do without it.

Annie Mae Hunt (1909–) of Dallas supported her family for twenty years as a seamstress and Avon saleswoman.

In a land of scarce water, the windmill was vital. "My job . . . was to climb the tower when there wasn't no wind. I had to turn the wheel by hand," said one West Texas woman.

Pioneer Families

The wholesale slaughter of the buffalo and the exile of the few remaining Native Americans to Oklahoma reservations in the 1870s cleared West Texas for settlement by white cattle ranchers.

It wasn't easy to live on the frontier. One girl who came to spend the summer on the Plains flew into a rage when she fell from the water wagon trying to fill a bucket. She exclaimed, "I hate a country where you have to dig for wood and climb for water." (Mesquite roots were dug for fuel, and water was hauled in barrels.)

Mary Ann Goodnight

Mary Ann "Molly" Goodnight and her husband Richard, along with Cornelia and John Adair, founded the famous J-A Ranch in the Texas Panhandle.

With the nearest neighbor seventy-five miles away, Molly had to provide her own social activities. She gave parties for the cowboys, taught them to read, wrote their letters, and patched their clothes. Her own loneliness was so great that when she received a gift of three chickens for Sunday dinner, she kept them as pets instead of cooking them. She wrote to her sister, "No one will ever know how much company those chickens were."

Lizzie Campbell, co-founder of the Matador Ranch, had no friends or relatives nearby to comfort her when she lost her baby daughter around 1886. She decided to keep the child's memory alive by gluing broken toys and favorite possessions onto a common water jug. It was called a "crazy jug."

Mary Ann "Molly" Goodnight (1839–1926) established the Panhandle's first ranch household in 1877 in the Palo Duro Canyon.

Mama would plant a hot bed of tomatoes for selling to others.
— Tilda Mae Bussey Holman

Women have raised food not only for their families but to sell as well. Farming was the work of the majority of Texas men and women until the 1940s. Women worked side by side with their husbands and children, fighting the same battles against the weather, trying to stay out of debt, and hoping for a good harvest. Raising garden produce or selling chickens, eggs, and butter were ways many farm women added to the family income.

"His wife was a good little woman and one of the sort that never tires. She usually milked 30 to 40 cows night and morning — and supplied the family, from butter and cheeses and chickens and eggs that she marketed in Galveston."
— "Reminiscences of C. C. Cox,"
describing Enuch Brunson's wife,
Mount Vernon, Texas, 1830s

Lizzie Thurman, Cooke County's first home demonstration agent, organized the Tomato Club in 1912.

Gardening could be an unexpected challenge. Snakes were among the hazards of a pioneer woman's life.

"My daddy . . . 'd been a cowman . . . when papa died in 1904 . . . Him and mama had 50 acres of land . . . she bought another 50 acres. That made her around 100 acres together. . . . My mother worked with the chickens and turkeys . . . Her and the girls . . . making coops and pens . . . Sometimes, we'd raise 75 or 80 turkeys, sometimes as many as a 100 . . . I'd bring the eggs into town . . . and I'd get a dime to twenty-five cents a dozen for them."
— Lulu V. Jones

Around 1900, Texas women began entering the paid labor force in greater numbers. By 1910, almost one-fourth of all women were working. Some were laundresses; others were farmers, schoolteachers, waitresses, and office clerks. The railroads, the waves of immigrants, and the money from cattle and cotton brought about urbanization in much of Texas, although most women still continued to live on farms. With the growth of towns, women found work in their own retail and service businesses, in telegraph and telephone companies, and in government and business offices.

YWCA

The Young Women's Christian Association was organized in Texas shortly after 1900; it helped women adjust from rural to city life. Young women new to the city were sometimes the targets of sexual harassment or economic exploitation. Many welcomed the protection of the "Y." A woman coming to Dallas after 1908 could rely on the YWCA for job training, bona fide employment offers, and a room. A "Y" for black women was organized in Houston in 1918 to give them a place to rest while in the downtown area. Originally a project of Methodist churchwomen and part of a national movement, the YWCA now represents women of every race and creed. It has always been managed completely by women.

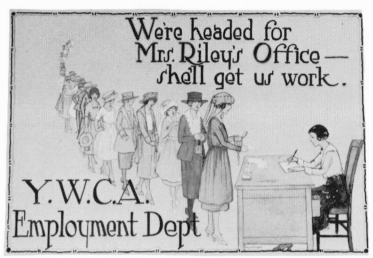

The Dallas YWCA opened in 1908.

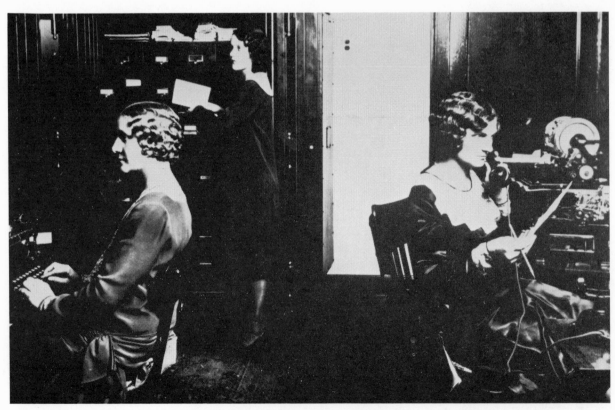

Plainview office workers around 1925. The occupation of secretary is still among the top ten for Texas women.

The Dallas main switchboard, 1919. In 1881, Miss Jennie Thompson became Dallas's first "telephonist."

The first Texas telephone exchange opened in Galveston in 1879. The first operators were young men who soon gained a reputation for being unreliable and rude. They were largely replaced by women by 1884. Among the early employees was Hattie Hutchison of Brazoria County who was in charge of that area's telephone office. She was ten years old.

The telephone company was one of the first "respectable" paid work settings for white women outside the home. The work was demanding; some operators in 1900 worked eleven to thirteen hours a day, seven days a week, and handled as many as 250 calls an hour — all for $15 to $25 a month. Still, working on the telephone company switchboard was cleaner and safer than many other jobs. Few women telephone operators ever advanced to high-level administrative positions in the early days. Most left when they got married, and those who stayed were usually promoted to other clerical positions within telephone exchanges.

Houston and San Antonio telephone operators went on strike in 1900 protesting long workdays and no days off or holidays. But it was not until 1938 that operators formed a union. About sixty percent of all workers joined these first locals of the Southwestern Bell Telephone Workers Union, organized along departmental lines. In 1947, all departments were organized into one local, and at the national level the Communications Workers of America united all telephone workers' unions. Today, ninety-five percent of all workers belong to the CWA. In Texas, CWA has 48,000 members and is the largest union in the state.

A few telephone systems were even owned by women. Suffrage leader Jessie Daniel Ames and her mother owned the system in Georgetown, and Mabel and Mavis Bird owned the telephone company in Panola County.

separate restrooms for female workers and adequate lighting and ventilation, but the legislation was rarely enforced.

Until World War II, most of the white working women were either single or widowed. It was not considered "socially acceptable" in many circles for married women to work outside the home. On the other hand, married black women have always composed a large segment of Texas's female work force. And in this early period, Hispanic women worked primarily in garment factories, as pecan shellers, migrant workers, laundresses, and domestics.

*Do you want a pure, blooming complexion?
If so, a few applications of Hogan's
MAGNOLIA BALM will gratify you. . . .
It makes a lady of Thirty Appear but Twenty.*
        Denison Daily News, September 27, 1879

Because so many Texas women began working around 1900, legislation was finally passed to mandate safe and clean working conditions. The Protection of Female Employees Act was adopted in 1918, at the urging of women's clubs. It required

Beauty Shops

As hats began going out of fashion, beauty shops became good businesses for women. The beauty shop had something for everyone. While white women had their hair curled on permanent wave machines, black women had their hair straightened with hot combs. Many Texas women earned a living by operating beauty shops in their homes.

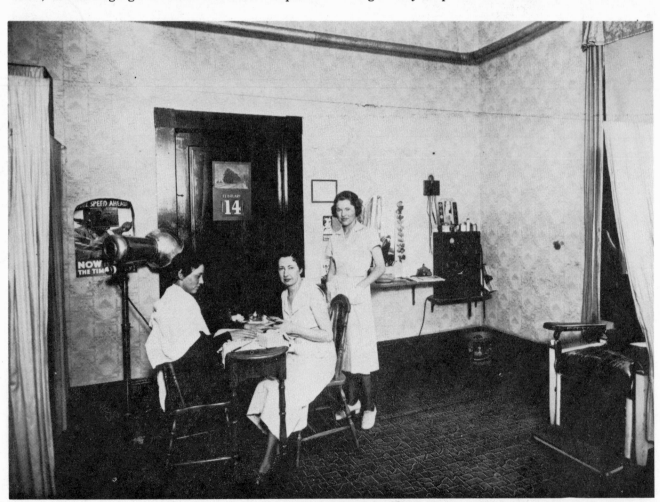

By 1950 Texas had more than 5,000 self-employed beauticians.

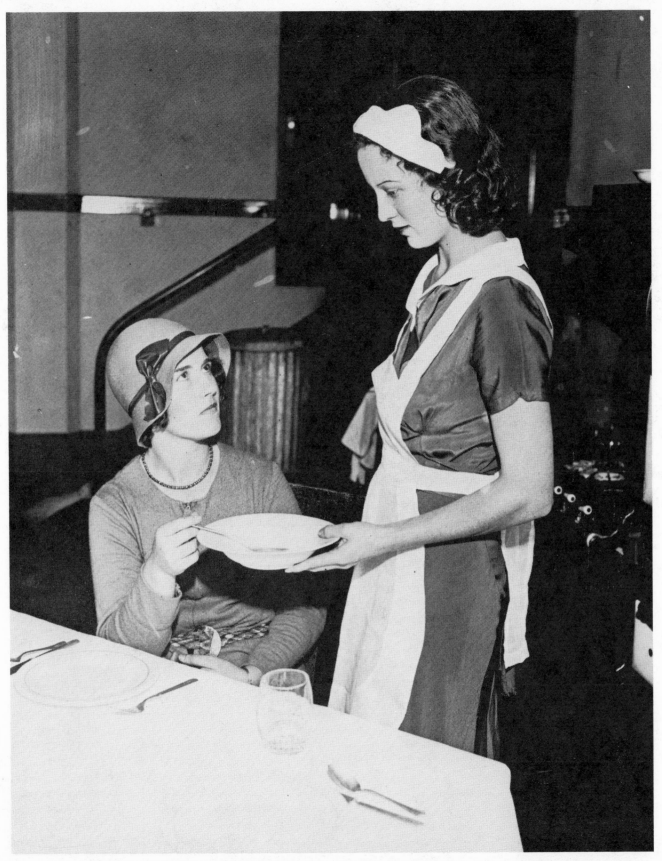

In 1880 and 1980 the occupations of working in a hotel, a restaurant, or in food services were among the top ten for Texas women.

Midwifery

Native American women in many Texas tribes were midwives. An elderly medicine woman and several others massaged the woman's abdomen and burned sage to purify the lodge during childbirth.

Women have always assisted each other at childbirth. Women having babies in early Texas settlements usually called for a local midwife like Doña María Perez of Sinton in San Patricio County. In the 1970s midwifery began enjoying a rebirth among Texas's expectant mothers.

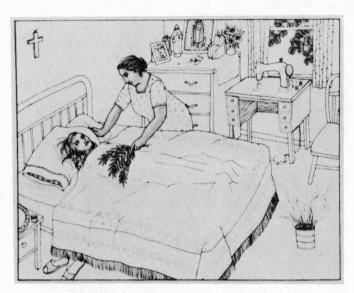

A curandera, *a traditional Hispanic folk healer, is featured in this etching by artist Carmen Lomas Garza.*

Elizabeth Boyle "Aunt Hank" Smith came to Crosbyton in 1877, where she was the only medical person within a 100-mile radius.

Before there were doctors in pioneer towns, women nursed children, cared for sick neighbors, and prepared and administered medicines.

Lay midwives pose with a public health nurse around 1922.

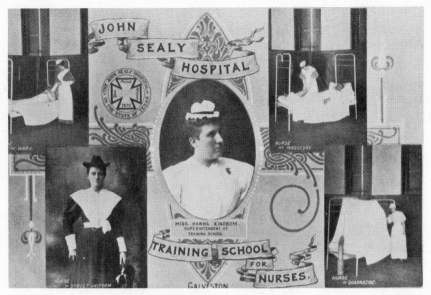

Texas's first nursing school was founded in 1890 at the John Sealy Hospital in Galveston.

Nursing began to be taken seriously as a profession in 1909 when the Texas Graduate Nurses Association persuaded the legislature to pass licensing standards. In 1985, there were 102,000 nurses registered in Texas.

Mary Coffee-Jones raised her family alone in Mount Pleasant. In her spare time, she read her son-in-law's medical books and began healing and delivering babies. At age seventy, in 1888, she moved to San Saba and continued healing. She helped organize the Union Church and often addressed the entire congregation.

Native American women healed with herbs and sometimes shared their knowledge with other frontier women. Margaret Hallett (1787–1863), the founder of Hallettsville, developed friendships with local Tonkawa women, who taught her to make medicine from herbs and nursed her through pneumonia.

Kezia de Pelchin from Arkansas pitched in when yellow fever hit Houston in 1878. She nursed the sick until the epidemic subsided; and by the end of 1883, she was head nurse of the city hospital. For five years, she tended the sick and campaigned for better facilities, conditions, and equipment.

A. Louise Dietrich

Louise Dietrich arrived in El Paso as a young graduate nurse in 1904. She was president of the Texas Graduate Nurses Association from 1912 to 1914 and spent a number of summers running the Baby Sanitarium in Cloudcroft, New Mexico.

Nurse A. Louise Dietrich (18??–1962) built her own maternity hospital in El Paso in 1910.

RULES FOR PIONEER TEACHERS

TEACHERS WILL NOT DRESS IN BRIGHT COLORS. AT LEAST TWO PETTICOATS MUST BE WORN, AND WILL BE DRIED IN PILLOWCASES.
TEACHERS WILL NOT MARRY OR KEEP COMPANY WITH MEN.
TEACHERS WILL NOT LOITER AT ICE CREAM STORES, SMOKE CIGARETTES, OR PLAY AT CARDS. SHE WILL NOT DYE HER HAIR UNDER ANY CIRCUMSTANCE. TEACHERS WILL ATTEND CHURCH EACH SUNDAY AND WILL NOT LEAVE TOWN AT ANY TIME WITHOUT PERMISSION OF THE CHAIRMAN OF THE SCHOOL BOARD.

Adina de Zavala (1861–1955) of San Antonio, the granddaughter of Lorenzo de Zavala, vice-president of the Texas Republic, was one of Texas's first women to get a degree in education (Sam Houston State Normal Institute, 1879).

Public Schools

Texas took a giant educational step ahead in 1875 by establishing a public school system, followed by a giant step backward in 1876 when a new state constitution required "separate but equal" facilities for black and white students. In 1889, Willie House was appointed Waco Superintendent of Schools, the first female in the South to hold that position.

By 1895 teaching had become a female profession in Texas when women outnumbered men 7,762 to 7,347. The average monthly salary for women teachers was $35.50 and for men, $49.20.

Many teachers devoted their whole lives to children. One Dallas teacher recalled that she kept working after her fiance threatened to leave her unless she quit. "I never saw him again." The year was 1890.

The U. S. Supreme Court decision in 1950 that blacks must be admitted to graduate programs at The University of Texas was followed closely by the decision in 1954, *Brown v. Board of Education*, which mandated desegregation of all public schools.

Students learn carpentry skills in the joinery shop of Dallas High School in 1908.

Dr. Annie Webb Blanton (1870–1945) was the first Texas woman to win statewide office when she was elected State Superintendent of Public Instruction in 1918. She served two terms.

The University of Texas at Austin

UT-Austin was coeducational when it opened in 1883. The first female student was Jessie Andrews (B.A. 1886), who became UT's first female instructor in 1888 in the German Department. In 1884, Helen Marr Kirby became the first woman on their administrative staff. Dr. Lorene Rogers, a chemist and nutritionist, was president from 1975 to 1979, the first woman to head a major coeducational U.S. university.

Annie Webb Blanton

Annie Webb Blanton won the office of State Superintendent of Public Instruction by 100,000 votes with the support of the Texas Equal Suffrage Association and women teachers. During her two terms she increased teachers' pay by over 50%, provided free textbooks, and improved schools for blacks and rural areas. She was vice-president of the National Education Association, the first female president of the Texas State Teachers Association, and the founder of Delta Kappa Gamma.

Dorothy Robinson described her forty-five year career in the East Texas public schools in her autobiography, The Bell Rings at Four: A Black Teacher's Chronicle of Change.

Dr. Mary Elizabeth Branch (1881–1944), as president of Austin's Tillotson College (1930–1944), led the struggle for quality education for black students.

Mary Elizabeth [Mrs. Lee] Bivins (1862–1951) was a civic leader and philanthropist who donated her home as a site for the Amarillo Public Library.

Historical Preservation

The Daughters of the Republic of Texas (DRT), founded in 1891 by Hally Ballinger Bryan and Betty Ballinger, have played an important role in historic preservation. They have cared for graves of Texas heroes, presented Texas flags and heroes' pictures to schools, sponsored school essay contests, restored historic buildings, and erected markers and monuments. In 1904, the DRT campaigned for the purchases of statues of Stephen F. Austin and Sam Houston by sculptor Elisabet Ney for placement in the state and national capitols.

Founders of Libraries

Women's clubs founded eighty-five percent of the libraries in Texas. The Texas Federation of Women's Clubs (TFWC) at its first statewide meeting in Tyler in 1898 launched a campaign to establish public libraries all across the state. They were very successful.

Mrs. J. C. Terrell of Fort Worth, as TFWC president, helped form the State Library Commission in 1898, and became known as the "Mother of Texas Libraries." In the beginning, women bought the books and served as volunteer librarians. Today, 230 of the state's 254 counties have at least one free public library.

Miss Mary Devana, aged 11 years, was awarded a handsome croquet set, having collected the most money — $18.65 — for the purchase of a library for the M. E. Church Sabbath school.
—*Denison Daily News*, July 8, 1879

Ada Simond (1903–) of Austin is a historian of the black experience and author of a series of children's books, Let's Pretend, Mae Dee and Her Family.

The reading room of Dallas's new Carnegie Library, founded by the Shakespeare Club under Mrs. Henry Exall in 1903.

Early Libraries

Odessa's first library was in the town jail. In Stephenville it was a room over a drugstore. Women started free public libraries wherever they could find the space — in a hotel, a courthouse basement, or the corner of an auto parts store. Retired teacher Lucía Madrid started a community library in the Presidio-Marfa area with 4,000 books in the corner of her family's general store.

Librarians

In 1894, Mary I. Stanton of El Paso opened a reading room for boys, one of the first children's libraries in the nation. Library science became a new profession for women around 1900. Julia Ideson became head of Houston's new Carnegie Library in 1903. A professional leader from the beginning, she was elected president of the Texas Library Association in 1910.

During World War I, Ideson organized a library for soldiers, worked for Liberty Loans, and went to France representing the American Library Association, for which she was later elected ALA vice-president. After the war, Ideson promoted successful bond issues to finance library facilities and campaigned for the first libraries for blacks in the South. Houston's downtown Julia Ideson Library is named in her honor.

Fannie Ratchford was director of the Rare Books Collections of The University of Texas at Austin for forty years and compiled the early writings of the Brontes. Much of her research was devoted to exposing literary forgeries.

The UT-Austin Latin American Library was named for its longtime director, Dr. Nettie Lee Benson; and Llerena Friend served as director of the UT-Austin Barker Texas History Center from 1950 to 1969.

Julia Ideson (1880–1945) graduated in the University of Texas's first class in library science in 1903.

Home demonstration agent Ada Collins Anderson (second from left) judges a hot roll contest for Kaufman County's 4-H Home Demonstration Club in 1946. Mrs. Anderson, of Austin, holds many civic and educational leadership offices.

Around 1900, many middle class homes began to change from centers of production to centers of consumption. New technology and new products were now available — indoor plumbing, gas stoves, electricity, washing machines, and ice for ice boxes. A new movement to professionalize the homemaker's role accompanied these changes. Domestic science, home economics, household engineering, and child psychology began to be taught.

Dr. Mary Gearing was a leader in this new movement. She inaugurated a school of domestic economy at The University of Texas at Austin. Under her leadership the school became the department of home economics, and in 1917 conferred its first degree of bachelor of science. Dr. Gearing was UT-Austin's first female chair of a department, serving for thirty-one years. She was the first woman on the faculty building committee and supervised the design of fifteen buildings.

Other universities have also played an important part in this movement. The Texas Woman's University has had a flourishing program since its opening in 1903. They have educated young women for homemaking, motherhood, and many professions. Dr. Kate Adele Hill, TWU's first PhD recipient and a national agricultural extension leader, wrote *Home Demonstration Work in Texas, 1915–1955*.

Domestic science came to rural areas in 1916 when Edna Trigg became Texas's first female home demonstration agent. Texas A&M University became the center for programs for white women when Maggie Barry founded the Home Demonstration Clubs of Texas in 1918. Prairie View A&M University was the center of programs for black women. Lucille Bishop Smith of their faculty invented the nation's first hot roll mix, and Dr. Jeffie O. A. Conner became the state's first black home demonstration agent (see page 105).

Dr. Mary E. Gearing (1872–1946) established one of the first public school home economics programs in the United States.

4

"MEN'S WORK" AND ENTREPRENEURISM

Texas history is full of examples of women who did jobs usually done by men. From Hispanic days, women were ranch owners and sometimes worked their own stock. Ex-schoolteachers Lizzie Johnson and Henrietta King were highly successful in the cattle business. In the 1840s Obedience Smith of Houston had a license to operate a dray. Mary Escher was a cotton checker on boats bound for Galveston after the Civil War. Mary Sweeney was an apothecary; Mollie Bailey ran a circus; and Sally Scull bought and sold horses and was a crack shot with a pistol in either hand. Around 1893, Dr. Sofie Herzog — a Vienna-trained physician and a mother of fourteen — came to Texas. She worked as a railroad doctor, and her specialty was digging out bullets.

Toward the end of the nineteenth century, Texas women began to train for professions considered the province of males, but progress was slow and sometimes painful. Henrietta Manlove Cunningham became the first registered woman pharmacist in the state in 1888, and in 1898, Dr. Mary Lou Shelman was certified by examination to practice dentistry. Two women were graduated from Texas medical schools in 1897 — Dr. Daisy Emery Allen and Dr. Marie Dietzel. A member of The University of Texas Board of Regents opined in 1933, "I think it is all right for women to study medicine, but I certainly would not encourage her [sic] to do it. . . . They cease largely to be women." As late as 1950, women were only five percent of the students at The University of Texas Medical Branch at Galveston; by 1984 they had reached twenty-eight percent.

Probably the first woman admitted to the Texas Bar was Hortense Ward in 1910. In 1970, women were still only eight percent of the law students at The University of Texas at Austin. By 1984, however, they were thirty-nine percent. Women are still greatly underrepresented in engineering and the sciences. Dr. Lorene Rogers, a chemist who in 1975 became president of The University of Texas at Austin, chose to work in the School of Home Economics when as a young PhD she was not offered equal treatment by the U. T. Chemistry Department.

Though Texas has been hard on women professionals, it has been somewhat more generous to women entrepreneurs. Governor E. J. Davis took out an ad in the Austin *Tri-Weekly Gazette* in 1871, advising readers to buy the pies of Mrs. Brown, a Negro, who had a stand near the capitol gate. From 1866 to 1899, a group of women in Belton called the Sanctificationists built up a chain of hotels by starting as domestic workers. Among the most successful of entrepreneurs have been Sarah Cockrell, capitalist, who owned much of downtown Dallas and built the first iron bridge across the Trinity River, and Ninfa Laurenzo, who parlayed a one-room tortilla factory into a chain of Mexican restaurants.

Some of the most adventuresome women in the world have worked in Texas. Early aviators Katherine and Marjorie Stinson had a flying school in San Antonio and trained pilots for World War I. During World War II, the Women's Airforce Service Pilots had their headquarters at Sweetwater, Texas; and today women astronauts are training at NASA in Houston and flying in space shuttles. Other Texas women have made their mark as journalists, activists, artists, politicians, outlaws, and entertainers.

Women entering the medical profession in Texas were subjected to ridicule. Dr. Leslie Waggener, president of The University of Texas, in an 1896 speech to the Texas Women's Press Association, warned: "I understand that many young women are looking forward to studying medicine ... and that already there is hardly a large city, even in the South, in which there are not one or two 'female doctors.' Against these personally I have not a word to say. But I deplore the effect of the example they set. The work of a doctor or surgeon is not work for a woman."

The first licensed female physicians in Texas received training elsewhere. Possibly the first to practice in Texas was Dr. Margaret Holland, a graduate of Chicago's Woman's Medical College in 1871, who set up an office in Houston. Dr. Josephine Kingsley, who came to San Antonio in 1878, was the city's first female physician, graduating from the University of Michigan in 1873.

The first two women medical graduates in Texas completed their studies in 1897. Dr. Daisy Emery Allen (1876–1958) graduated from Fort Worth University Medical School second in her class, and Dr. Marie Delalondre Dietzel, from The University of Texas at Galveston Medical School. Dr. Hallie Earle practiced in Waco until age eighty-three (1911–1963), still the only female physician in town. H. EARLE, M.S., M.D., INTERNIST read her shingle.

As late as 1950, women were only five percent of the students at the University of Texas Medical Branch in Galveston. By 1984, they constituted twenty-eight percent.

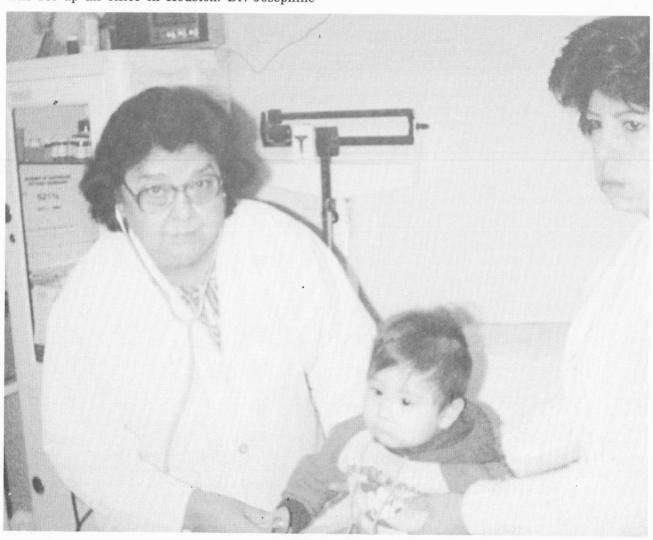

Dr. Clotilde P. Garcia (1917–), one of the first Mexican-Americans in Texas to enter the medical profession, has delivered more than 8,000 babies in Corpus Christi, written books on Hispanic history, and worked on numerous educational, health, and civic endeavors.

Dr. Sofie Herzog (1848–1925) of Brazoria was Chief Surgeon for the St. Louis, Brownsville, and Mexico Railroad from 1907 to 1925.

Dr. Connie Yerwood was the first black physician on the staff of the Texas Department of Health from 1936 to 1977.

Dr. Sofie Herzog

Dr. Sofie Herzog, a widowed mother of fourteen, moved to the small Texas coastal community of Brazoria in 1895. She shocked the local townspeople by riding astride her horse, dressed in a split skirt and a man's hat.

Dr. Herzog had an unlikely profession. As surgeon for the St. Louis, Brownsville, and Mexico Railroad for almost twenty years, she often rode handcars, boxcars, and engines to reach her suffering patients. Local townspeople got used to seeing Dr. Sofie whizzing by, holding on to her hat with one hand and her doctor's bag with the other.

Bandits, feuds, political scraps, and free-for-alls combined to create business for Dr. Herzog. A large number of her first cases came from digging bullets out of wounded men. She wore a necklace made of twenty-four souvenir slugs (which she had extracted) strung between gold links. She insisted the necklace brought her good luck, and she wore it constantly. At her request, she was buried with it.

> I think it is all right for women to study medicine, but I certainly would not encourage her to do it. . . . They cease largely to be women. They simply cannot follow the profession of medicine and be a wife and mother.
> —Dr. Kenneth Aynesworth, U.T. Board of Regents, The University of Texas, 1933

Dr. Connie Yerwood

In 1983, Dr. Connie Yerwood of Austin was honored for fifty years of service to mankind by the Meharry Medical College. She was on the staff of the Texas State Department of Health for over forty years.

Dr. Yerwood was one of the first black female doctors in Texas. Her father was a physician and her mother a teacher. She graduated cum laude, as a Doctor of Medicine, from Meharry Medical College in Nashville, Tennessee, in 1933, at a time when blacks were not admitted to Texas medical schools. She interned at Kansas City General Hospital and trained in public health at the University of Michigan.

Dr. Yerwood joined the staff of the Texas Department of Health in 1936. She worked in the Division of Maternal and Child Health, setting up immunization programs for children, establishing prenatal and family planning clinics for expectant mothers, and training midwives. Dr. Yerwood faced discrimination as a black woman repeatedly when staff members with less experience were promoted above her until the Civil Rights Act of 1964. She was then promoted to director of Maternal and Child Health Services, a position she held until her retirement in 1977.

A special All-Woman Supreme Court appointed by Governor Pat M. Neff in 1925 made the New York Times. *(Left to right) Justice Hattie Henenberg, Chief Justice Hortense Ward, and Justice Ruth Brazzil.*

The All-Woman Supreme Court, 1925

In 1925, Governor Pat Neff appointed three women to serve as justices of a special Texas Supreme Court because the presiding male justices were all members of a fraternal organization involved in the case to be heard. The governor feared a potential conflict of interest.

Frances Cox (Mrs. J. Pinckney) Henderson (1820–1897) was the first woman to practice law in Texas.

The first all-woman state supreme court in the U.S. had as its chief justice Hortense Ward (1875–1944) of Houston, said to be the first Texas woman admitted to the bar in 1910. Ward wrote the Married Women's Property Rights Bill, which became law in 1913. Hattie Henenberg (1896–1974), one of the other two members, was an assistant district attorney and organized the Dallas Bar Association.

Frances Cox Henderson

Frances Cox Henderson, the first woman to practice law in Texas, had been a child prodigy in mathematics, music, and languages. She studied in Paris, France, from 1829 to 1839 where she met and married J. Pinckney Henderson, the Republic of Texas ambassador to France (and later the new state's first governor in 1845). The couple settled in San Augustine, Texas, where Henderson continued her studies. She ran the law office and handled cases when her husband and his law partners were out of town.

After the Civil War and her husband's death, Frances became interested in the freed slaves and wrote the novel *Prissell Baker, Freedwoman,* translating it into seventeen languages. She later moved to New Jersey, where she founded a home for aged women and a welfare society.

Sarah T. Hughes

Sarah T. Hughes from Baltimore was a judge in Texas for forty years. She was first elected to the Texas House of Representatives as a Democrat from Dallas in 1931 and voted Most Valuable Member during her second term.

Hughes became Texas's first female judge when appointed to the Fourteenth District Court in 1935 by Governor James Allred. She was reelected district judge seven times but lost a 1946 race for the U. S. Congress.

Judge Hughes was the national president of the Federation of Business and Professional Women's Clubs in 1952. They spearheaded her nomination for the vice-presidency on the Democratic Party ticket — the first woman ever —but Hughes withdrew her name. Hughes was an early advocate for women's rights; she wrote the bill that in 1954 finally gave women the right to serve on Texas juries.

Judge Hughes headed the Dallas United Nations Association in the 1950s. She was Dallas County Cochairman, Kennedy–Johnson campaign in 1960 and was appointed by President John F. Kennedy as Texas's first female federal judge, Northern District, in 1961. After Kennedy's assassination in 1963, she administered the Presidential oath of office to Vice-President Lyndon B. Johnson.

Judge Sarah T. Hughes (1896–1985) was Texas's first female state judge, appointed to a district courtship in 1935 by Governor James Allred. President John F. Kennedy appointed her to the federal bench in 1961.

Judge Gabrielle McDonald of Houston became the first black federal judge in Texas in 1979, and only the third black woman in the U. S. to hold such a position.

In 1983, Judge Elma Salinas of Laredo became the first Mexican-American woman appointed to a district court bench in the history of Texas and the U.S. She was elected to a full term in 1984.

Ruby Sondock and Sandra Day O'Connor

Ruby Sondock, a Houston district judge since 1977, became the Texas Supreme Court's first female justice in 1982, appointed by Governor Bill Clements to fill a six-month unexpired term. Sandra Day O'Connor, born in El Paso, was appointed as the first woman to the U. S. Supreme Court in 1981 by President Ronald Reagan.

Dr. Mary Sophie Young

Dr. Mary Sophie Young was a distinguished botanist who came to The University of Texas at Austin in 1910 and was promoted to instructor the next year. She was in charge of the herbarium from 1912 to 1919, and taught a course in taxonomy. Dr. Young, an avid plant collector, wrote two books about her findings in the Austin area.

Young made numerous field trips each summer from 1914 to 1918 to the wildest and most mountainous sections of West Texas, bringing back hundreds of plant specimens. An excerpt from her 1914 journal follows:

> There are no trails in these mountains. . . . Back of us was a cliff several hundred feet high. . . . Botanically it was quite different from anything else I have seen. It was beautifully painted with orange, yellow, and gray lichens, and decorated in every crevice with very many plants, ferns, selaginellas, liverworts . . . a tangle of grapevines, wild tobacco (?) mentzelia. . . . The view before us was certainly magnificent — the foothills in the foreground, with our canyons winding out through rolling green hills to the plains beyond. *There* was space; . . . the plain lay before us, stretching out miles and miles to the mountains, which like gray clouds skirted the horizon.

Dr. Mary Sophie Young (1872–1919), a pioneer in the field of plant classification, is shown on a summer field trip to West Texas, about 1914.

Although the scientific community has been slow to accept women, a number of individuals have done distinguished work and blazed trails for those to follow.

The first state botanist, in 1872, and author of the state's first botany textbook was Maud Jeannie Young. Helen Selina King was an entomologist whose studies on insects were published in the *American Naturalist* in 1878. In 1890, Elizabeth Sthreshley of Austin invented and patented a typewriter for the blind called the punctograph. She sold the state twelve machines for $1000.

The only woman in the U. S. working for a state geological survey in 1938 was Helen Plummer, a consulting paleontologist for the Texas Bureau of Economic Geology. After World War II, Dr. Dora Struther, a former Women's Airforce Service Pilot, became Chief of Human Factors Engineering for Bell Helicopter Textron and wrote over 200 articles. Dr. Pauline Mack, a national expert in textiles and nutrition, headed the Texas Woman's University Research Institute from 1962 to 1983. She won an award for her studies in bone density for NASA's Skylab program.

Ynés Mexia de Reyades (1870–1938) was an international botanical collector who discovered 500 new specimens. Fifty species are named in her honor.

Ynés Mexia de Reyades

Ynés Mexia de Reyades from Mexia was an international collector of botanical specimens from 1922 to 1937. She collected approximately 145,000 specimens in Mexico, Alaska, and South America. They are housed at the Bancroft Library, University of California at Berkeley.

Dr. Ellen D. Furey was the first full-time pathologist at San Antonio's Robert B. Green Hospital, 1939.

In 1939, Mrs. S. A. Masterson took over her husband's business, becoming San Antonio's only female commercial photographer.

Some Texas women have been well-known and effective as writers. It was women's "propaganda" (Mary Austin Holley, Jane Cazneau, and Elise Waerenskjold) that brought many early settlers to the state. Mrs. E. Spann of Galveston edited Texas's first literary journal, *The Texian Monthly Magazine*, in 1858. In fact, almost one-third of the first forty literary magazines in Texas were published by women.

In 1893, reporters and writers organized the Texas Women's Press Association as an alternative to the male-dominated professional organization. The group entered twenty-seven volumes of the writing of Texas women at the Women's World Fair in Washington, D.C., in 1895. The work of 119 female writers in Texas was being published at that time. The national headquarters of Women in Communications, founded in 1909, is in Austin.

Women were prominent in founding the Poetry Society of Texas in 1921. Of the ten poets laureate between 1932 and 1954, six were women. Still other women did interesting work — though not for publication — including memoirs, letters, and journals.

Journalists

Lydia Starr McPherson (18?? – 1903) and Dorothy Renick (190?? – 1967)

Lydia Starr McPherson started one of the state's earliest newspapers, the *Whitesboro Democrat*, in 1877. She and her husband had previously run the *Oklahoma Star* in Caddo territory in 1874, with one page set in the Choctaw language. She began publishing the *Sherman Democrat* in 1879, still in existence. She was a delegate to the World's Press Convention and an Honorary Commissioner of the World's Exposition at New Orleans in 1885. She was the local postmistress, and her poetry appeared frequently in *Cosmopolitan*.

Dorothy Renick dreamed of being a reporter, but her father, like so many other parents, advised her to teach school. "You'll be surer of three meals a day," he said. Dorothy was the first "regular" female reporter for the *Waco Times-Herald* in the 1920s. Although she faced ridicule from the old-timers who scoffed at college-trained journalists, she soon made a reputation of her own. In 1924, she left for New York.

Clara McLaughlin was the first black woman in the U. S. to own a television station when she launched the East Texas Television Network in 1984.

Clara McLaughlin

Clara McLaughlin is the first black female in the U. S. to own a television station. Her goal is to open three additional stations as part of her East Texas Television Network. In 1984, she launched KLMG, a CBS affiliate, in Longview. A resident of Houston, she commutes twice a week. "I listened to people with experience because I wanted to be Number One." A graduate of Howard University, she and her husband wrote *The Black Parent's Handbook: A Guide to Healthy Pregnancy, Birth, and Child Care.*

Jovita Idár (1885–1946) (second from right), a noted Laredo journalist, blocked the doorway of the newspaper El Progresso in 1914 to keep Texas Rangers from closing it. The paper had printed an article criticizing President Woodrow Wilson's dispatch of U.S. troops to the Texas border.

I write mainly for the race of women . . . I am their sister . . . if my experience can help any sad or doubtful woman to outleap her own shadow, and to stand bravely out in the sunshine to meet her destiny, whatever it may be, I shall have done well.
— Amelia Barr, *All the Days of My Life*

Amelia Barr

From 1883 to 1919, Amelia Barr was one of the nation's most prolific and popular novelists. She and her husband had earlier lived in Austin (1856–1866) where she ran a seminary for young ladies, clerked for the Confederate Tax Assessors, and kept a diary. Barr's autobiography, *All the Days of My Life*, considered one of the best of the eighty-one volumes of her work, contains many details about her life in Texas.

After the war and the loss of her husband and sons, Barr moved to New York with her daughters. She supported them by writing more than 1,000 articles and poems and later novels. Her 1885 novel, *Jan Vedder's Wife*, established her reputation. Her book *Remember the Alamo* was well-known in Texas. She wrote her last novel at the age of eighty-seven.

Amelia Barr (1831–1919) described Austin from 1856 to 1866 in her autobiography All the Days of My Life.

Selma Metzenthin-Raunick, born in Berlin, was a historian of German Texas writers. She published poetry and prose in German, as well as magazine articles about German Texas settlements.

Lucy Ella Gonzales Parsons (1853–1942) from Waco was a leader of the Chicago working class movement, a writer, an editor, and an orator.

She is a self-possessed speaker and fluent . . .
Waco Daily Examiner, May 9, 1886

Lucy Parsons of Waco was one Texas woman who achieved national and international attention for her fifty years of radical writings and political activities. She published newspapers, books, and pamphlets; led demonstrations; and was an impassioned orator. Lucy Parsons was a leader of the Chicago Working Women's Union and a founder of the Industrial Workers of the World. In 1886, she organized sewing women into the Knights of Labor to strike for the eight-hour day.

After the Civil War, Lucy married Albert Parsons, also of Waco, a white ex-Confederate Scout turned Radical Republican. In 1870, Albert moved to Austin to become Secretary to the Texas Senate, where his brother was a state senator. During Reconstruction there was hostility toward couples of mixed marriage; in 1873, Lucy and Albert moved to Chicago, where they became leaders of the working class movement.

Lucy Parsons's first published work was a poem in the *Socialist*. She was also a writer for *The Alarm*, an anarchist paper. Child labor was prevalent in Chicago, and Lucy condemned it in one of her powerful articles, "The Factory Child, their Wrongs Portrayed and their Rescue Demanded."

In 1886, Albert was one of eight anarchists arrested in connection with what became known as the Haymarket Affair. Lucy's legal battle to free her husband and the others failed. Albert and three of the men were hanged, despite national protests. In 1893, Illinois Governor Peter Altgeld pardoned those still in prison and condemned the judicial errors and prejudicial evidence which had convicted them.

The mother of two children, Lucy Parsons was a strong believer in the nuclear family, which she saw as the ideal form in a free Socialist society. She wrote that women would be emancipated only when wage slavery under capitalism was ended: "It is woman's economical dependence which makes her enslavement to man possible."

Katherine Ann Porter (1892–1980)

Katherine Ann Porter wrote her first novel at the age of six and her second at the age of seventy-one — *Ship of Fools*. It earned her $1 million and the Pulitzer Prize and was made into a movie with Vivien Leigh and Lee Marvin. She left Texas at the age of eighteen because, "I didn't want to be regarded as a freak; that was how they regarded women who tried to write. I had to make a revolt, a rebellion."

Maud Cuney-Hare

Maud Cuney-Hare had to go as far away as Boston to obtain a good education in music because Texas schools were officially segregated in the 1890s. Her father, Norris Wright Cuney, was a leading Texas Republican at that time. Maud's parents sent her to the New England Conservatory, where she also had to fight against racial discrimination. "I refused to leave the dormitory. . . . I insisted upon proper treatment," she said.

In 1893, Maud visited night schools in Cambridge and wrote her father, suggesting such schools would be good for Galveston. He succeeded in getting three free night schools for that city. Maud Cuney-Hare published a biography of her father, as well as the historic landmark *Negro Musicians and Their Music*. After graduation, she moved back to Texas for a brief time and directed music at the Deaf, Dumb, and Blind Institute for Colored Youth. She returned to Boston where she made her permanent home.

Maud Cuney-Hare (1874–1936) of Galveston was a noted music historian, folklorist, pianist, and playwright.

Estela Portillo Trambley and Jovita Gonzales de Mireles

Estela Portillo Trambley is one of the nation's foremost contemporary Chicana poets, short story writers, and playwrights. In 1973, she won the Quinto Sol Literary Prize for her plays *Day of the Swallows* and *Sun Images*. Her play *Sor Juana [Ines de la Cruz]* deals with the life of the celebrated Mexican nun, feminist, and thinker of the seventeenth century.

Jovita Gonzales de Mireles (1899 – 1983) of Corpus Christi and her husband Edmundo were probably the first Texas educators to use Spanish-language textbooks in the public schools. They established a bilingual program in Corpus Christi in the 1940s. Mrs. Mireles, a noted folklorist as well, was the first Mexican-American to be president of the Texas Folklore Society. She wrote "After the Barbed Wire Came Hunger."

Frances Sanger Mossiker (1906 – 1985)

Frances Sanger Mossiker of Dallas was the author of numerous nonfiction books which explored the glamour, excitement, and intrigue of European royalty. Her first book, *The Queen's Necklace* about Marie Antoinette, earned her the Carr P. Collins nonfiction award of the Texas Institute of Letters in 1961 — a first for a woman and for a book not about the Southwest.

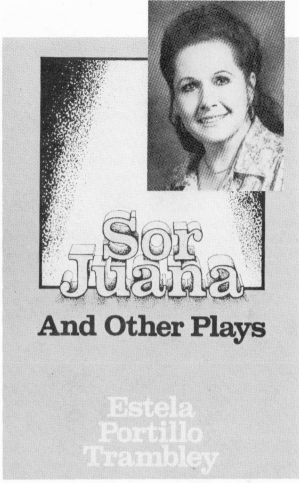

The cover of *Sor Juana* [Ines de la Cruz] *and Other Plays, written by Estela Portillo Trambley of El Paso.*

Dorothy Scarborough

Dorothy Scarborough's novel, *The Wind* was originally banned in Sweetwater in 1925 because it was considered uncomplimentary to that city. It was made into an MGM movie starring Lillian Gish. Scarborough began the first college journalism course in Texas as an instructor at Baylor University (1905–1916), was president of the Texas Folklore Society in 1916, and was on the Columbia University faculty from 1917 to 1935.

Scarborough wrote for the *New York Sun* from 1917 to 1918. She published many books with Texas settings, including *In the Land of Cotton* (about the plight of tenant farmers) and *Impatient Griselda* (three stereotypes of Texas women). A champion of women's rights, Scarborough's novel, *The Woman's Viewpoint*, in 1925, dealt with women's roles and discrimination against women.

Dr. Dorothy Scarborough (1878 – 1935) of Waco was the author of many novels with Texas settings, including The Wind, *a controversial portrayal of life in West Texas.*

Texas women have run small businesses from pioneer days. They used their domestic skills to run boardinghouses, dressmaking shops, laundries, and restaurants. Other women started and developed larger enterprises.

In 1982, Mary Kay Cosmetics, Texas's top performer on the New York Stock Exchange, employed 200,000 female beauty consultants. Enid Justin, the world's first female bootmaker, began working in her father's boot factory at age twelve. In 1925, she founded the Nocona Boot Company. At first there was resistance to buying boots made by a woman, but today her products are worn throughout the world. Irene Cox Wischer of San Antonio heads three petroleum companies which specialize in oil exploration and development. Her Pinto Pipeline Company's servicing equipment is painted pink. In 1954, Mary Moody Northen of Galveston was president of more than fifty corporations.

Ninfa Laurenzo

Ninfa Laurenzo and her husband ran Houston's Rio Grande Food Products for many years. She took over the business after his death in 1969, set up ten tables in her tortilla shop, and with a vision of the future, called it a restaurant.

Soon her popular menus and tasty food led to expansion. By the end of 1981, there were twenty restaurants with projected sales of $30 million. Especially known for her Tacos al Carbón, Ninfa's is now a major restaurant chain.

Corinne De Viney, standing beside her two-ton truck at the Union Stockyards in San Antonio in 1939, was the only licensed woman livestock truck operator in Caldwell County.

Selling lemonade in the summertime.

Mrs. C. J. Washmon of Mesquite poses in front of her family-owned grocery store.

Florence Butt

Florence Butt's original sixty dollar investment in 1905 has grown into the twelfth largest grocery chain in the U.S. — the H.E.B. Corporation. She and her husband moved to Kerrville thinking the dry climate would cure his tuberculosis. To support her family, which by then included three young sons, Mrs. Butt knocked on doors soliciting customers for her A & P grocery products. One woman slammed the door in her face, saying, "I don't buy from peddlers." Mrs. Butt was deeply hurt by this rejection, but economic need drove her on.

She rented a two-story building for nine dollars a month, moved her family upstairs, and opened a grocery store on the ground floor. Her sons delivered orders, first in a baby carriage and, as they prospered, with a horse and wagon. Her hard work and good business sense resulted in a highly successful corporation.

Florence Butt (1864–1954) was the founder of the twelfth largest grocery chain in the U. S. — the H. E. B. Corporation.

Since the days when Native Americans beaded their dresses and moccasins and tattooed their bodies, Texas women have been interested in fashion, clothing, and makeup.

Many were successful turn-of-the-century merchandisers like Mrs. A. W. Rysinger and Miss Josephine Theis, who opened businesses in their own home town. More recently, women like Idelle Rabin of Dallas have achieved recognition for creative retailing. Rabin, the owner of Delann's, was awarded the 1985 Golden Sun Award by the Southwest Apparel Manufacturers Association.

Mrs. A. W. Rysinger, the owner of Austin's Central Millinery Emporium, supplied custom hats and dresses to black women from 1907 to 1911.

In the early 1900s, Austin women shopped at Miss Josephine Theis's millinery shop in the downtown area.

Mrs. Neiman created the world-famous Neiman-Marcus style by insisting on simple ornamentation, the best fabrics, and quality workmanship. She waited on her customers personally, and many would not think of making a purchase without her approval.

Carrie Neiman became chair of the board in 1950, but she continued waiting on her favored customers. A woman of understated elegance, she always wore black, a strand of pearls, and two gold bracelets.

Elsie Frankfurt

Elsie Frankfurt thought her pregnant sister looked like an unmade bed in her oversized clothes. She designed a maternity skirt cut out over the tummy in 1939, borrowed $500, and went into business with her sisters Edna and Louise. Their Page Boy Company was such a success that others clamored for the fashion. The firm's first style show was held in 1947 at New York's Stork Club. In 1951, Elsie Frankfurt became the first woman to be inducted into the Young Presidents Organization, of which all executives of million-dollar corporations were under the age of forty. In 1952, she won *Mademoiselle*'s Merit Award.

Carrie Marcus Neiman (1883–1953) was a co-founder of Dallas's world-famous Neiman-Marcus Department Store in 1907.

Carrie Marcus Neiman

Carrie Marcus Neiman brought high fashion to Texas. She had been the top saleswoman at a Dallas department store when she joined her brother in Atlanta, Georgia, in 1905 for sales promotion work. They turned down the Coca-Cola franchise, preferring fashion to fizz, and returned to open a new Dallas department store, Neiman-Marcus. They believed ready-to-wear would soon replace custom apparel, and they were right.

The Frankfurt sisters of Dallas, led by Elsie, founded the Page Boy Company to sell fashionable maternity wear. (Left to right) Edna, Louise, and Elsie Frankfurt.

Bette Graham (1922–1980) (third from right, holding shovel), the inventor of Liquid Paper, breaks ground in 1968 for her first corporate headquarters in Dallas.

Lucille Bishop Smith (1892–1985), a Prairie View A&M home economics professor, developed the first hot roll mix in the U. S., founded a family corporation at the age of eighty-two, and set up the first Commercial Foods Department at the college level.

Texas women invented highly successful commercial products and set up corporations to market them.

Bette Graham

Bette Graham's invention of Liquid Paper correction fluid would have been sufficient to assure her place in American history and in the hearts of secretaries.

When electric typewriters were introduced, it was difficult to correct mistakes. Graham realized an artist could paint over her mistakes, so why not paint over typing errors? Experimenting in her kitchen with an old-fashioned mixmaster, she invented Liquid Paper in 1951. IBM declined her offer to sell them the product, so she started her own business, marketing Liquid Paper through a trade journal.

By 1967 Liquid Paper was a multimillion dollar firm, and in 1975 Graham opened an international headquarters in Dallas. In 1976, she retired as chair of the board and established the Bette Clair McMurry Foundation and later the Gihon Foundation to help women in the work force. Both were among the nation's first private philanthropic organizations devoted primarily to helping women. In 1979, she sold the corporation for $47.5 million.

Bette Graham was more than an inventor. As a secretary and single mother, she overcame tremendous obstacles to become an artist, entrepreneur, and philanthropist. She was not content to accumulate wealth. "I want to see my money working for people," she said.

Sarah Horton Cockrell (1819–1892) (inset) was Dallas's first capitalist whose many businesses included the successful Todd Mills.

Marcella Perry is one of Texas's most successful women bankers. She is president of Houston's Heights Savings, a $300 million company with 110 employees and twelve branches.

Sarah Horton Cockrell

In 1852, Alex Cockrell came home and told his wife, "Mrs. Cockrell, I have bought you a town." The town was Dallas. Sarah was Alex's business partner and adviser since he was illiterate.

When Alex was killed in 1858 over a debt, Sarah, a widow with four young children, collected the debt and took charge of the business. After the wooden bridge Alex had built across the Trinity collapsed, Sarah organized a corporation and built an iron bridge instead. In 1872, she purchased a one-third interest in Dallas's first flour mill; by 1877 sales were $3 million.

Sarah Cockrell's conservative business philosophy set the tone for later generations of Dallas entrepreneurs. The *Dallas City Directory* listed her occupation as Capitalist. When she died, she owned one-fourth of downtown Dallas and acreage in surrounding counties. Her will was so lengthy it was published in pamphlet form. She was undoubtedly Dallas's richest citizen for many years.

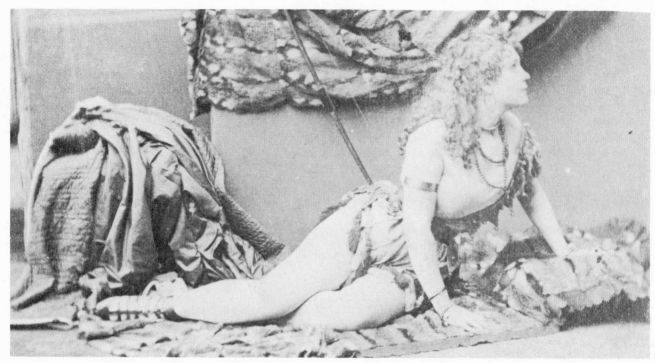

Adah Isaacs Menken (1835–1868), known as the Naked Lady from Nacogdoches, became America's first sex symbol when she appeared on the New York stage in a flesh-colored body stocking in 1860.

The first theatrical company toured Texas in 1838. The hit of the 1850s was a ballet company starring Adah Menken, later to receive international acclaim as "The Naked Lady from Nacogdoches."

A hundred years later, the Margo Jones Theatre in Dallas (1947–1959) hit the national spotlight as the home of one of the first theaters-in-the-round in the United States. Jones established her theater on the State Fairgrounds soon after codirecting the original production of *The Glass Menagerie* by Tennessee Williams on Broadway. Pioneering in arena staging, Jones produced the premiers of Williams's *Summer and Smoke* and Jerome Lawrence and Robert Lee's *Inherit the Wind.*

Numerous stars of the stage, screen, and television have come from Texas. They include Mary Martin, Debbie Allen, Vikki Carr, Cyd Charisse, Ann Miller, Linda Darnell, Carol Burnett, Janis Joplin, and Academy Award winners Ginger Rogers and Sissy Spacek.

Sandy Duncan of Tyler, shown here in Paramount's Star Spangled Girl, *is often remembered for her Broadway portrayal of* Peter Pan.

Etta Moten

When George Gershwin wrote the role of Bess in *Porgy and Bess*, it is said Etta Moten was the performer he had in mind. Her interpretation of that (1942–1945) Broadway role remains one of the most memorable. Her other Broadway performances were *Sugar Hill* and *Lysistrata*.

Etta Moten sang in her father's church choir in San Antonio as a child. She produced radio shows in Kansas and during the Harlem Renaissance, went to New York. She made two movie musicals: *Flying Down to Rio* with Ginger Rogers and Fred Astaire and *The Gold Diggers of 1933* with Joan Blondell and Dick Powell, in which she sang the featured song, "My Forgotten Man." In 1934, she was invited to the White House to sing for President Franklin D. and Mrs. Eleanor Roosevelt.

Moten is a popular lecturer on Africa and the Afro-American heritage and has been a delegate to many international conferences, including International Woman's Year in Mexico City in 1975 and the United Nations Mid-Decade Conference of Women in Copenhagen in 1980. At age eighty, she talked about keeping up-to-date: "The only difference between a rut and a grave is depth, and I'm not ready for either one."

THE AMERICAN NIGHTINGALE
JOSEPHINE
LUCCHESE
COLORATURA SOPRANO

Philadelphia Pa.

Etta Moten (1901–) was a stage and screen performer who became famous for her starring role in Porgy and Bess *in the 1940s.*

Josephine Lucchese (1901–1974)

Josephine Lucchese of San Antonio was an internationally acclaimed opera singer and one of the world's foremost coloratura sopranos, who performed for thirty-five years (1922–1957). She made many Grand Tours of Europe and was prima donna of the Philadelphia Opera Company. Lucchese was a member of the music faculty of The University of Texas at Austin from 1957 to 1970.

Estella Maxey

Estella Maxey was a child prodigy who played for services at Waco's Second Baptist Church. She later gave piano lessons for affluent black children, but the Depression soon had its impact on such luxuries.

After marriage to Nathaniel Maxey, a saxophonist, her orchestra "Stella and Her Boys" became the most popular in town. They entertained white Waco society at parties and afternoon dances. Waco was still segregated, and blacks could not attend. During World War II, the orchestra prospered by playing at nearby military posts. Estella Maxey died young, and Waco named a public housing project in her honor.

Rosa Dominguez was a popular San Antonio singer on WCAR radio station in 1925.

Estella Maxey (1908–1948) was a musical prodigy who organized an orchestra which became Waco's most popular entertainment during World War II.

Mollie Bailey (1844–1918), the Circus Queen of the Southwest, toured Texas towns for thirty years.

Mollie A. Bailey

Mollie Bailey's Circus, the only one in the world owned by a woman, traveled by wagon and later by train to Texas towns for over thirty years.

In 1885, Mollie and her husband Gus moved to Texas from Alabama. They organized a one-ring tent circus which soon grew to thirty-one wagons and 200 animals. Their six children were all part of the business. When Gus died in 1896, Mollie ran the flourishing circus until her death.

Mollie Bailey was warm and generous. She gave money to charity, lent her 100 lots for ball games and camp meetings, and let children and Confederate veterans in free. One West Texas town balked at the presence of her black cook; she raged at the sheriff and never returned. A friend of Comanche Chief Quanah Parker, Mollie wintered in Dallas and Houston. When the spring came, the magic cry was, "Aunt Mollie's coming!"

Horseback Riding

Horseback riding for women is a Texas tradition. In 1849, W. Steinert recorded, "We saw a small five- to six-year-old Negro girl working a large American horse quite skillfully."

Mary Bunton wrote in her autobiography *A Bride on the Chisholm Trail*: "I was the first woman to ride astride in our part of the State, and you may be sure it caused a stampede among the cowboys and the cattle."

Texas women like Sydna Yokley Woodward, Tad Lucas, and Nancy Binford have excelled as rodeo stars. They have taken their riding skills into the workplace as well. Nancy Binford and her mother Katherine own a flourishing ranch in the Texas Panhandle. Other women are employed at the Amarillo livestock auction to pen the cattle after they are sold. This highly skilled work requires each young woman to handle about 10,000 — sometimes very temperamental — cattle per week. Because of their superior skill, more women than men are employed.

Texas women like Sydna Yokley Woodward have excelled as rodeo stars.

Small Texas towns have avidly followed their girls' teams since the turn of the century. The myth that competitive sports harmed young girls caused school officials to stop organized girls' basketball programs in the 1920s. But sports fans prevailed, and girls' basketball was revived. Today more than 25,000 Texas high school girls play Interscholastic League basketball.

The Lady Longhorns

The Lady Longhorn basketball team of The University of Texas at Austin has dominated Southwest Conference Competition for years. In 1986, they captured the NCAA women's basketball championship.

Jody Conradt, coach since 1976, was voted National Coach of the Year in 1984 by the Women's Basketball Coaches Association. Coach Conradt is proud she has not lost an athlete for academic reasons.

Outstanding players have included Annette Smith, Linda Waggoner, Kamie Ethridge, and Clarissa Davis.

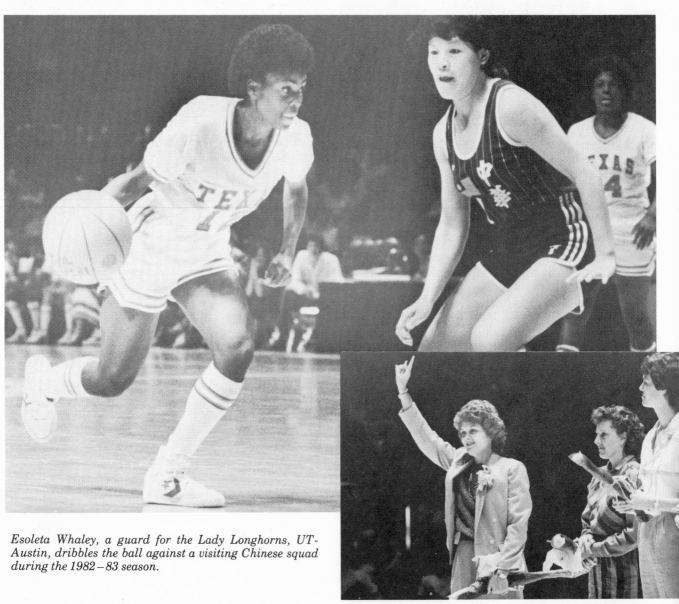

Esoleta Whaley, a guard for the Lady Longhorns, UT-Austin, dribbles the ball against a visiting Chinese squad during the 1982–83 season.

Jody Conradt (left), Lady Longhorns coach, voted National Coach of the Year in 1984, with her assistant coaches, Lynn Pool and Jill Rankin.

Babe Didrikson Zaharias (1914–1956) (right) of Beaumont set more records, won more medals, and swept more tournaments than any other twentieth century athlete, male or female.

Babe Didrikson Zaharias transformed people's ideas about female athletes forever. She combined unique physical abilities with fierce competitive fire and a deep confidence in herself.

Babe grew up in Beaumont playing sandlot baseball with the boys. Her mother had been a Norwegian ice skating champion; her four older brothers excelled in sports. Babe's father, a carpenter, built his children backyard gym equipment. Babe set up her own hurdling course by jumping neighborhood hedges.

Her initial successes in Beaumont high school sports were met with encouragement by her parents. She excelled in basketball, though she entered all the sports. She was recruited to play for the Golden Cyclones girls' basketball team of the Employers Casualty Company in Dallas and led them to victory, earning all-American honors in 1930, 1931, and 1932.

Babe's boss introduced her to track and field competition. She competed in the Amateur Athletic Union National Meets in 1932 as a one-woman team and won all the events. At the 1932 Olympic Games in Los Angeles, she broke the world record in javelin by fourteen feet on her first throw of 143 feet, four inches. She took the gold medal. She also broke the eighty-meter hurdle world record and earned the gold medal. She won the silver medal in high jump in a controversial decision. She became the toast of America.

Perhaps Babe received her greatest acclaim on the golf course. She won eighty-two tournaments as both an amateur and a professional. In 1946–1947, as an amateur, she won seventeen tournaments in a row. She turned professional and was instrumental in the formation of the Ladies Professional Golf Association (LPGA).

Babe Didrikson's stature as a versatile athletic competitor gained her recognition by newspaper reporters as the top woman athlete of the first half of the twentieth century. Although her life was cut short by cancer, she gave her best and climbed the heights of success. The Babe Didrikson Museum in Beaumont honors her.

Katherine Stinson (1891–1972) of San Antonio was the greatest woman pilot in her day. She was best known for her daring stunt and endurance flights.

Katherine Stinson was never afraid to fly "because I had confidence in myself and my plane," she said.

Katherine soloed first in 1912 — eleven years before Charles Lindbergh ever climbed into a cockpit — and she helped the pioneer aviation industry gain public acceptance. She was history's first night skywriter and the first woman to loop-the-loop. The petite, one hundred-pound brunette captured the public's imagination as she set distance and endurance records. Her flights over San Antonio in an open-air Wright Model-B plane called attention to that city's ideal climate conditions that later propelled it into becoming a major aviation center. She joined her sister Marjorie, also a pilot, and their mother in opening a flying school in San Antonio, Stinson Field.

Katherine's reputation for courage and daring spread to Japan and China, where she traveled for exhibition flights. More than 25,000 people turned out in 1916 in Yokohama to watch her skywrite with fireworks, and the Japanese women hailed her as their liberator.

In 1917, Katherine set a world long-distance record, flying from San Diego to San Francisco nonstop — 610 miles in nine hours and ten minutes. She had flown longer and covered more miles than any other aviator in the world, man or woman.

Katherine was a good mechanic, as well as a good pilot. Despite the teasing she sometimes received from male pilots because she went over every inch of her plane, scrubbing and polishing the wires and cleaning the joints, she persisted.

When World War I began, Katherine raised over $2 million for the Red Cross through fund-raising flights. She volunteered for military duty but was turned down because she was a woman. Instead she flew the first scheduled airmail service between Washington, D. C. and New York. She went to France as an ambulance driver. After the war, she moved to New Mexico for her health and became an award-winning architect.

94

Wouldn't it be great when I'm old and gray to be able to lean back in my rocking chair and remember when I was out taking a stroll among the stars?

— Dr. Shannon Lucid

America's first astronauts were men. For the first sixteen years of the space program, beginning in 1961, space exploration was off-limits to women. In 1977, the National Aeronautics and Space Administration (NASA) in Houston began recruiting women and minorities into the space program under the Equal Employment Opportunity Act of 1972. More than 1,000 of the 8,000 applicants that year were women. Of the thirty-five new astronauts selected for training between 1978 and 1980, eight were women.

The eight female astronauts in the program in 1984 were highly trained and experienced in their fields. Three were engineers (Dr. Mary Cleave, Bonnie Dunbar, and Dr. Judith Resnik, who was lost aboard *Challenger* in 1986); two were physicians (Dr. Anna Fisher, with a background in chemistry and emergency medicine, and Dr. Rhea Seddon, a nutritionist); one was a biochemist (Dr. Shannon Lucid); and two were physicists (Dr. Sally Ride and Dr. Kathryn D. Sullivan).

In 1983, Dr. Sally Ride was a member of the Space Shuttle Challenger crew. She operated the remote manipulator arm, used for the first time; released a satellite into orbit; and then retrieved it. In 1984, Dr. Kathryn Sullivan became the first U. S. woman to walk in space.

In 1983, Dr. Sally Ride made history when she became the first U. S. woman in space, orbiting earth 231 times.

95

Miss Eco's Fountain *by Chelo Amezcua (1903–1975) of Del Rio, was drawn with ballpoint pens, the only artist's tools she could afford. She worked as a dime store clerk while perfecting her Texas filigree art and finally achieved national recognition.*

5

CLUBS AND CIVIC ACTIVITIES

The forty years between 1880 and 1920 saw a marked expansion from the domestic into the public sphere of the activities of Texas women. Starting with missionary societies and church and synagogue auxiliaries, they moved on to organize politically, masterminding many major reforms. Without the efforts of club women and women as philanthropists, Texas would have no child labor laws, no welfare system, no reform schools, no compulsory education. We would not have most of the familiar apparatus of civilization — our libraries, museums, schools, symphonies, or even the wildflowers along the roads.

The first time Texas women organized politically, it was to stop the sale of whiskey. Temperance women saw drinking linked to social ills such as spouse and child abuse; they believed prohibition could save the family, reduce crime, and end poverty. Participation in the Woman's Christian Temperance Union gave them the courage and experience to speak in public, collect petitions, and publish newspapers. Mrs. J. B. Beauchamp (Marshall), for instance, a minister's wife, was a "quiet little woman" until she accepted the post of WCTU president. She spent four years traveling more than 5,000 miles by train, lecturing, and organizing; and she launched a successful campaign to get young boys removed from Rusk penitentiary and placed in a new boys' reformatory at Gatesville. Temperance women also sought the vote to further their goals.

Women organized early for self-improvement, too. In 1898, the Current Topics Club of El Paso studied: George Eliot, *A Doll's House* by Henrik Ibsen, Household Economics from the Standpoint of the Mistress and the Maid, Roman History, Sanitation, Can Criminals Be Reclaimed, Cooperative Living, and Women as Rulers. Under leaders like Eleanor Brackenridge of San Antonio, study clubs became "department clubs" that also embraced community action. The Texas Federation of Women's Clubs was involved in founding eighty-five percent of the state's public libraries. They lobbied through a wide variety of measures such as compulsory school attendance, pure food inspection, and a juvenile court system. They had projects to help children, the poor, and minorities; and they preserved and celebrated Texas's history.

Other significant organizations included the Texas Congress of Mothers (later PTA), which got sanitary drinking fountains mandated for public schools; the Texas Association of Colored Women, which worked to improve conditions for their community; the National Council of Jewish Women, which stressed literacy projects and kindergartens; La Liga Femeníl Mexicanista, which was both political and educational; and the Texas Graduate Nurses Association, which got licensing for their profession.

After women got the vote, they didn't stop working. For example, housewives organized to buy Texas products and called for standards for movie houses; the League of Women Voters informed voters; the American Association of University Women and the League of United Latin American Citizens gave scholarships; the National Association for the Advancement of Colored People worked on issues of justice; and Junior Leagues and garden clubs, too, worked to enhance the quality of life.

Helen Stoddard (1850–1941) of Fort Worth was a temperance leader, lobbyist, and the author of legislation which established what is now Texas Woman's University in Denton.

Woman's Christian Temperance Union (WCTU)

They were called the White Ribbon Army. The Woman's Christian Temperance Union, founded in 1882 in Paris, Texas, was the first organized political movement of Texas women. Alcohol and family abuse had become a major problem in Texas after the Civil War. When national WCTU organizer Frances Willard spoke in Paris, she found women there ready to work for the adoption of the Eighteenth Amendment (prohibition) to the U.S. Constitution. In 1918, the Texas Legislature ratified the amendment. It took effect in 1920, but was repealed in 1933.

The WCTU had an influence far beyond its work for prohibition. It was the first organization to endorse women's suffrage (1887); it led the women to tackle many other social issues; and possibly most important, it taught them to organize, speak in public, and lobby. Black women had their own WCTU chapters. Mothers Against Drunk Driving (MADD), headquartered in Dallas, is a contemporary spinoff from the earlier work of the WCTU.

Helen Stoddard

Helen Stoddard, a mathematics professor, took up temperance work after hearing national WCTU leader Mrs. Anna Palmer in Dallas in 1887. As WCTU's legislative chair, Stoddard secured the passage of the "Scientific Temperance Instruction Bill" for teaching about alcohol and narcotics in the public schools. She was influential in the passage of an anti-cigarette law, a pure food law, and an anti-child labor law. Stoddard was elected WCTU's third president, served for sixteen years (1891–1907), and traveled extensively in Texas and abroad, organizing world WCTU congresses.

Lufkin Woman's Christian Temperance Union parade in 1915. The signs read: GIVE US CLEAN MEN *and* THINK OF YOUR MOTHER.

A young woman needs more than fitness for the home, since from choice or otherwise she may never have a home of her own. She must be fitted for an independent life ... thoroughly equipped in some congenial, self-supporting, commercial business.... A lack of economic freedom has heretofore made marriage often only a commercial contract.

—Helen Stoddard, 1903

The Texas Woman's University in Denton opened in 1903. Its first name was the Texas Industrial Institute and College for the Education of the White Girls of the State of Texas in Arts and Sciences.

The fight to establish the school took ten years of hard work by the Woman's Christian Temperance Union, led by their president, Helen Stoddard. Those opposing its establishment claimed that "instinct will make a woman a perfect housekeeper, a model wife, a wise mother." Some legislators even said that if girls were taught to earn a living, they would cease getting married and within fifty years there wouldn't be a baby born in the state. But the WCTU and Stoddard had a different view. They believed all worthy young women should have an opportunity for a college education. Stoddard said, "A practical knowledge of doing some definite thing well would be the best protection that a parent could give his daughter.

Stoddard, Eleanor Brackenridge, and Mrs. Cone Johnson were appointed to the new school's first board of regents, the first Texas women to serve on a college board. It took seventy years before TWU had a woman president. Dr. Mary Evelyn Blagg Huey was appointed in 1976.

One of the first students in a science laboratory at the Texas Woman's University in Denton.

Young black women could prepare themselves for the teaching profession at Samuel Huston College in Austin, a co-educational, Methodist school which opened in 1900. It later merged with Tillotson College.

Viola Case (1821–1894) founded Texas's first women's club in 1873, the Victoria Literary Society. The club's first president was an eleven-year-old student at Mrs. Case's Victoria Female Academy.

Mrs. Percy V. (Anna) Pennybacker (1861–1938) of Austin was the national president of the General Federation of Women's Clubs from 1912 to 1916.

Texas Federation of Women's Clubs (TFWC)

In 1899, two years after its formation, the Texas Federation of Women's Clubs, an interdenominational organization, dropped the word *literary* from its name. Members gradually expanded their programs from cultural self-enrichment to difficult social issues. This coalition involving thousands of women had a profound impact upon social reform in Texas.

Among the TFWC's first priorities were the establishment of public libraries and educational reform (see page 66). At that time, Texas had no compulsory school attendance law. In 1907, the TFWC got enacted into law the establishment of a juvenile court, the designation of wife and child desertion as a felony, regulation of child adoption, public kindergartens, marital blood tests, and guardianship laws for divorced women.

Anna [Mrs. Percy V.] Pennybacker

Anna Pennybacker was a distinguished author, club woman, and world peace advocate. She was president of the TFWC (1901–1903) and the only Texan elected president of the national body, the General Federation of Women's Clubs (1912–1916). She visited every state in the union, plus Alaska and Cuba.

An educator and master storyteller, Mrs. Pennybacker self-published, with her husband, the state's first Texas history textbook in 1888. It became a standard reference, soon selling 30,000 copies annually.

Despite pacifist leanings, Mrs. Pennybacker supported World War I, but with misgivings. In 1918, this mother of four wrote, "I feel with all the strength of my woman's being that war is a relic of barbarism."

After the war, Pennybacker worked hard for international peace and cooperation. She represented three newspapers at the League of Nations from 1925 to 1931, chaired the Woman's Committee for Near East Relief, and traveled on behalf of the International Council of Women. She supported a Disarmament Conference in 1932, and advocated U. S. membership in the World Court and the ratification of the Kellogg–Briand Pact outlawing war as an instrument of national policy.

The Douglass Club of Austin was organized in 1906 by Laura Pierce to study literature and do philanthropic work.

Black Women's Club Movement

Because the Texas Federation of Women's Clubs was segregated, black women formed their own organizations. In 1905, the Texas Association of Colored Women (TACW) was founded in Gainesville by Mrs. M. E. Y. Moore. For years the TACW campaigned for a state-financed home for delinquent Negro girls, which was approved by the legislature in 1927 but not funded until 1945.

Many social clubs sprang up among black women, like the King's Daughters, the Eastern Stars of the Masonic Lodges, and sororities. These clubs were concerned with self-improvement, as well as community service. They raised funds for scholarships, voter registration, and tutoring.

Seven black women's social clubs organized the Community Welfare Association of Austin in 1927, and plunged into an ambitious service program. They established a community center which housed a nursery school, a well-baby clinic, and a milk distribution center. They also provided meeting rooms for parent education classes.

In the 1930s, black Houston women organized scouting for Negro girls, the first such program in the South. Mrs. B. J. Covington was one of Houston's foremost civic leaders. She was the first chair of the Blue Triangle YWCA, state chair of the Texas Commission on Interracial Cooperation, and a member of the city's first Anna Dupree Negro Child Center Board. Her husband was a Houston heart specialist for over fifty years, and their home was open to nationally-known blacks (such as Booker T. Washington and Marian Anderson), who were excluded from local hotels during segregation.

Black women organized mothers' clubs like Jack and Jill of America to stimulate child growth and development. Stung by discrimination, many black women also organized to fight for their political and civil rights (see pages 117, 128).

Madison County women organized to collect poll taxes and work for better public facilities. In 1935, Houston's Black Women for Social Change protested injustices against their citizens. Texas chapters of the National Council of Negro Women were formed around 1946. The Dallas chapter hosted an appearance by national founder Mrs. Mary McLeod Bethune in 1948. The Austin chapter sponsored a panel discussion, "Minority Women in Action," with speakers from Mexico and from the National Council of Jewish Women, in 1947. LINKS, INC., a national women's organization founded in 1946, is dedicated to the promotion of civic, cultural, and educational activities.

MARY ELEANOR BRACKENRIDGE

Women's clubs are no longer amusing; they are the solemn rising of the good women of the land who organize to stand together as a unit to work for high purposes. And with them to aid and bless and encourage, are all good men.

These sentiments of Eleanor Brackenridge exemplified the club woman at her best. She founded the first Texas women's club with separate departments in 1898, after returning from the Fourth General Federation of Women's Clubs Convention in Denver. Through her efforts, hundreds of clubs around the state were founded.

Brackenridge was president of the San Antonio Women's Club for seven years. It studied laws affecting women and children and got industrial and manual training into the public schools and a police matron and probation officers hired at city hall.

A socialite who lived with her mother and never married, Brackenridge was a founder of the Texas Congress of Mothers (later the PTA). She wrote and published a pamphlet, "The Legal Status of Women in Texas" (ca. 1911), which influenced legislation regarding married women's property rights.

Brackenridge revitalized the Texas suffrage movement, which had lain dormant since 1905. In 1913, she was elected president of the Texas Woman Suffrage Association; within a year it had twenty-one local chapters and 2,500 members. Her exceptional abilities helped to insure its eventual success. A temperance leader as well, she worked for the establishment of Texas Woman's University and was one of three women on its first board of regents.

Mary Eleanor Brackenridge (1837–1924) of San Antonio was one of the first women in the United States to serve on a bank board. She was a temperance and suffrage leader.

Clara Driscoll

Clara Driscoll, the fiery daughter of a millionaire South Texas rancher, became a successful author, playwright, politician, diplomat, philanthropist, and businesswoman. As a young woman, she traveled to New York and made the grand tour of Europe. Upon her return, she joined the fight to save the Alamo. She wrote two novels and a comic opera about Mexico which had a successful Broadway run.

A generous benefactor of the Texas Federation of Women's Clubs, Driscoll paid off their building debt of $92,000. She left a fortune to establish the free and nonsectarian Driscoll Foundation Children's Hospital in Corpus Christi. When she died, *Time* wrote, "Politicians learned to respect her. She could drink, cuss, and connive with the best of them, outspend practically all of them."

Clara Driscoll (1881–1945) of Corpus Christi and Austin, whose $25,000 checks saved the Alamo, was a writer, diplomat, politician, and philanthropist.

Anna Hertzberg

Anna Hertzberg formed a club when she saw a problem or wanted to get something done. She started the Tuesday Music Club to sponsor concerts and scholarships, and organized an association which launched San Antonio's first symphony. She was a founder of the San Antonio Women's Club, which started the city's first public library.

As president of the San Antonio Council of Jewish Women, Hertzberg established the city's first night school and sold the idea to the school board. Councils of Jewish Women in other cities were active in community service as well. The Dallas Council established that city's first free milk fund (still in existence) and provided "penny lunches" for poor school children until the public schools opened lunchrooms.

For thirty-five years, Hertzberg succeeded at almost every type of club work. Under her leadership as president from 1911 to 1913, the Texas Federation of Women's Clubs influenced the passage of laws protecting married women's property rights. She was president of the Texas Kindergarten Association and even got elected to the San Antonio School Board in 1915, years before women got the vote. She also chaired the Texas Commission of the Panama Pacific International Exposition.

Anna Hertzberg (1862–1937) of San Antonio was president of the Tuesday Music Club, vice-president of the National Council of Jewish Women, and a founder of the San Antonio Symphony Orchestra.

Vol. 8　July, 1912　No. 2

OFFICIAL ORGAN OF THE TEXAS CONGRESS OF MOTHERS
Mouthpiece Conference for Education and State University Extension

commission, pure food inspection, a juvenile court system, public kindergartens, child labor and compulsory school attendance laws, a bureau of child hygiene, and funds for a division of child welfare.

In 1918, Mrs. Claude De Van Watts was appointed Texas's first child welfare inspector and chief of the first Texas Department of Labor. During her four-year term, she worked for the passage of twenty-two laws which improved working conditions.

Individual mothers' clubs and PTAs have enriched schools in their communities in countless ways. For example, the Crockett Parent-Teachers Club in San Antonio, organized in 1902, furnished books, benches, pictures, a victrola, and chairs. They raised money to build a restroom in the school and a free clinic. PTAs today continue this tradition of dedicated service to schoolchildren.

Ella Caruthers Porter (18?? – 1939) of Hillsboro founded and served as the first president of the Texas Congress of Mothers (later PTA) in 1909.

Mothers' Clubs and PTAs

Mothers' Clubs were organized to stop the practice of hiring children as young as ten to work in the fields, cotton mills, and kitchens. The Dallas Mothers' Club was formed in 1895, and Mrs. George B. Dealey was the founder. This was two years before the National Congress in 1897. They were prompted by unsanitary conditions on school grounds and in buildings. Mrs. P. P. Tucker and Mrs. E. P. Turner were elected to the Dallas Board of Education in 1908, ten years before women got the right to vote in Texas.

The Texas Congress of Mothers was founded by Ella Caruthers Porter in 1909, after she attended the first International Congress on Child Welfare in Washington, D. C. Porter's interest in children was long-standing; as chair of the Mothers Department, Woman's Christian Temperance Union, Porter had attended a world conference in Scotland in 1900.

Under Porter's leadership from 1909 to 1917, the Texas Congress of Mothers (which later became the Parent Teacher Association) was one of the women's groups that lobbied successfully to get laws and programs passed for the benefit of women and children. Legislation included a state child welfare

Dr. Jeffie O. A. Conner (1895–1972) of Waco was a club leader, home demonstration agent, educator, and statewide civic leader.

Jovita Idár (1885–1946) of Laredo and San Antonio was a writer, teacher, and feminist who organized La Liga Femenil Mexicanista in 1911 to promote the rights of Mexican-Americans and women.

Dr. Jeffie O. A. Conner

Dr. Jeffie Conner was president of the Texas Association of Colored Women from 1956 to 1958. The TACW purchased and ran a home for delinquent girls, worked for better public accommodations for blacks (such as on trains), and purchased a camp for Negro girls near Alvarado.

Dr. Conner was employed by the U. S. Department of Agriculture from 1923 until 1948 as their first black home demonstration agent in Texas and finally as district supervisor for seventeen counties. She was then appointed supervisor of the McLennan County public schools.

Dr. Conner's leadership extended into many other areas of public life. She was a member of the Race Relations Commission of Texas and the Texas Committee on Public School Education.

Jovita Idár

Jovita Idár founded La Liga Femenil Mexicanista (The League of Mexican Women) in 1911 at a meeting of El Primér Congreso Mexicanista in Laredo. One speaker lectured against lynching. Another speaker favored education for women equal to that of men, quoting, "Educate a woman and you educate a family." La Liga's first project was providing free instruction for poor Mexican-American children. Idár wrote for *La Crónica* (owned by her father) and *El Progresso*, Spanish-language papers which condemned violence against South Texas Mexican-Americans (see page 77).

When the Mexican Revolution (which began in 1910) reached Laredo, Idár and Leonór Villegas de Magnón organized La Cruz Blanca (the White Cross), putting aside their careers to nurse soldiers (see page 119).

Jovita Idár moved to San Antonio in 1917, where she started a free kindergarten and edited a Methodist Spanish-language paper, *El Heraldo Cristiano*. She inspired a whole generation of women after her:

"Sister teacher, you . . . have seen flashes of light budding in the eyes of some children and have felt the pleasure of understanding that you have opened the doors of knowledge for a human being."

Dominique de Menil of Houston is a patron of the arts.

Texas has had hundreds of women philanthropists whose generous donations of funds have been responsible for the creation and maintenance of museums, hospitals, colleges, nursery schools, and all manner of public and private institutions. Mary Moody Northen of Galveston has shaped dozens of Texas communities as head of the Moody Foundation which has funded libraries, school and college buildings, museums, and medical centers all across the state.

Anna Dupree

Anna Dupree was a successful Houston beautician who shared her wealth with her community. Mrs. Dupree and her husband, C. A. Dupree, invested wisely and owned a chain of black businesses. They began giving their money away. They established one of Texas's first orphanages for black children in 1944 — the Anna Dupree Cottage of the Negro Child Center. They also established the Johnson Home for the Aged and helped fund the first permanent building at Texas Southern University.

Dominique de Menil

Dominique de Menil (1909–) was another Houston benefactor. She and her husband John initiated more innovative arts projects than anyone else in that city. "The enjoyment of having beautiful canvases on the wall was what first guided our purchases," says this woman of rare vision and generosity.

The couple funded the Art History Department at the University of St. Thomas, a Media Center at Rice University, and the Rothko Chapel, as well as major donations to the Museum of Fine Arts. In 1986, a new museum — the Menil Collection — was opened to house their 10,000 art objects, one of the most extensive collections in the world.

Anna Dupree (1829–1977) of Houston was a successful beautician who became a generous philanthropist, donating funds for a home for dependent black children and for other institutions and projects.

In 1904, a group of Austin citizens united with the German Aid Society to construct the Altenheim (German for "Home for the Aged") for elderly women.

Homes for the Aged and Children

Texas women have founded numerous social welfare institutions to care for those unable to care for themselves. In 1894, black Austin women formed the Heart's Ease Circle which built the King's Daughters Home for the Aged. The need was so great that another Austinite built the Nancy Scott Home for Decrepit Old Women. Dallas's first interfaith activity among women was the establishment of an annual "Silver Tea" to benefit a nonsectarian old ladies' home.

Edna Gladney (1880–1961)

Answering a desperate but long-ignored need, Edna Gladney ran the Texas Children's Home in Fort Worth from 1925 to 1960. Later called the Edna Gladney Home, it was Texas's first agency to provide services for unwed mothers and adoptive homes for children. Gladney objected to the social stigma attached to children born out of wedlock, and her lobbying forced the legislature to pass laws erasing the word *illegitimate* from birth certificates. The Edna Gladney Home was immortalized by Greer Garson in the film *Blossoms in the Dust*.

Mrs. George (Kate) Ripley (????–1976)

Another related need was met when Kate Ripley, a Dallas club leader, and her husband George broke the law to help women. They founded Texas's first Family Planning and Birth Control Center in 1935 at a time when the federal Comstock Law made it illegal to provide women with birth control information or devices.

The Ripleys became friends of the national birth control crusader Margaret Sanger. They sent Sanger empty packing boxes from their shirt factory, and Sanger returned them filled with diaphragms. The nation's first public meeting to discuss birth control was arranged by Kate Ripley; she also got a Margaret Sanger Day designated at the Texas Centennial.

When the Comstock Law was struck down by the U. S. Supreme Court in 1936, women all over Texas followed Kate Ripley's lead in establishing planned parenthood centers. Twenty-five years later, Ginny Whitehill, another Dallas woman, began working with Planned Parenthood as a Junior League volunteer. She explained, "My initial introduction to the women's movement was through my concern for children. It is my conviction that babies are so miraculous that they deserve to come to parents who want them."

Lady Bird Johnson (1912–) of Washington and Austin has led the nation in beautification, conservation, and wildflower research.

Lady Bird Johnson

While she served as First Lady from 1963 to 1968, Lady Bird Johnson, the wife of President Lyndon B. Johnson, assumed a leadership position as a conservationist. She was the driving force behind the passage of the 1965 Highway Beautification Act and received the nation's highest civilian award, the Medal of Freedom.

Mrs. Johnson's most recent project has been the establishment in 1982 of the National Wildflower Research Center. She gave sixty acres of prime land along the Colorado River near Austin, together with $125,000, for its creation. She said, "I want to encourage the wildflowers' use and thereby preserve a piece of our natural heritage. Turn to the native, indigenous things that require less water and no fertilizer, less maintenance, no herbicides, no mowing, mostly just less manpower."

The Tradition of Texas Women

Claudia Alta (Taylor) Johnson is one of a long line of Texas women concerned about the land. The Colonial Dames of America got the bluebonnet named the Texas state flower in 1903, and club woman Sallie Ward Beretta led a successful statewide effort to plant bluebonnet seeds along Texas highways in the 1920s. In 1924, Emily Edwards and the San Antonio Conservation Society used a puppet show to dramatize the issues and persuaded the city commission to drop plans to pave over the San Antonio River as a drainage ditch. The river was saved, and today San Antonio is unique among America's cities. Its river is a major tourist attraction. Bess Heard, a pioneer conservationist, founded the Heard Natural Science Museum in McKinney in 1967.

Many Texas museums came into being because women saved or preserved books, letters, photographs, art, or historical records. Suffrage leader Annette Finnigan (1873–1940) gave her collection of Egyptian and Greek antiquities to Houston's Museum of Fine Arts. Other women founded art centers and museums, and symphony orchestras.

Ima Hogg

" . . . that music may reach and touch every facet of our civic life."

Ima Hogg was the driving force in the cultural life of Houston for over sixty years. A philanthropist who used her family wealth to benefit her community, she founded the Houston Symphony, established the Houston Child Guidance Clinic, and with her brother Will funded the Hogg Foundation for Mental Health.

Ima Hogg developed a sense of community service early. As the young daughter of Governor Jim Hogg, she traveled with him to many state institutions. She was elected to the Houston School Board in 1943; she worked hard to equalize the salaries of men and women, blacks and whites.

Miss Hogg was a renowned collector of American decorative arts. In addition to donating her home Bayou Bend which was filled with priceless antiques to the City of Houston, she personally supervised the restoration of the Winedale Historical Center in Round Top and gave it to UT-Austin as an outdoor museum and music center.

Music was always part of Ima Hogg's life. She studied piano in New York and Europe and in later life composed dissonant music and admired the work of the Beatles. On her ninetieth birthday, the Houston Symphony featured pianist Artur Rubinstein, and honored her with a special concert. She made her last trip abroad at the age of ninety-three — to visit museums and attend concerts. She died in London.

Ima Hogg (1882–1975) of Houston helped found the Houston Symphony in 1913 and with her brother Will established the Hogg Foundation for Mental Health.

In 1966 Ima Hogg donated her elegant mansion Bayou Bend, filled with Early American decorative arts, to Houston's Museum of Fine Arts.

6

THE FIGHT FOR DEMOCRACY

Texas women have been involved in political activity for over one hundred years. They sent representatives to the Reconstruction Convention of 1868 demanding the vote. A delegate from Burleson County, T. H. Mundine, introduced a women's suffrage resolution, and a majority of the Committee on State Affairs recommended its adoption. But the Convention voted it down, 52–13. At the Constitutional Convention of 1875, delegates introduced two women's suffrage resolutions, and Mrs. G. W. Hyatt of Eldorado submitted a petition. The resolutions and the petition were ignored.

In 1873, women joined the Grange, a movement to help farm families. In 1879, a black woman, Madam Walker, was reported by the *Denison Daily News* to have traveled around the state speaking on the "Political Destiny of the Colored Race in the U. S." By 1900, Hispanic women were caught up in the events preceding the Mexican Revolution of 1910.

The first Texas women's group to endorse women's suffrage was the WCTU in 1887. Many local option elections were held regarding the sale of alcohol, but resistance to prohibition was strong. Temperance members decided they needed the vote to achieve prohibition, and many became leading suffragists. The suffrage movement had several waves of development. The final push required a new organization, the Texas Equal Suffrage Association, founded in 1915. Black and brown women, as well as whites, worked for suffrage, but not within the same organizations. Women won an interim measure in 1918 when they won the right to vote in the ruling party's (Democratic) primary. In 1919, the Texas Legislature ratified the Nineteenth (women's suffrage) Amendment to the U. S. Constitution; the federal amendment took effect in 1920.

In the 1920s and 1930s, women began running for and winning political office. By 1933 six women had been elected to the state legislature, and Miriam A. (Ma) Ferguson was a two-time Texas governor. The Petticoat Lobby, a coalition of women's clubs, secured passage of its entire legislative program.

During the Great Depression some women organized unions and led strikes. Other women and women's clubs opened soup kitchens and initiated a whole host of welfare measures.

Since World War II, many Texans have been active in politics, the civil rights movement, and the women's movement. Juanita Craft organized almost 200 chapters of the NAACP; Christia Adair integrated Houston's public facilities; and women like Dorothy Turner and Velma Roberts of Austin fought hard for equity. Vilma Martinez, an attorney, was director of the Mexican American Legal Defense and Education Fund and a key figure in the passage of the Voting Rights Act of 1965.

Continuous efforts by women, despite ridicule of their aims, have won many uphill fights for legal equality. The Married Women's Property Act of 1913 allowed women to own their earnings, but not until 1954 could women serve on juries. The Texas Marital Property Act of 1967, which improved the legal status of married women, was drafted by Louise B. Raggio; and in 1972 Texas voters approved the Texas Equal Legal Rights Amendment by four to one.

Who Represents Her?

IF a woman is responsible for an accident, if she defaults on her contracts, if she slanders her neighbors, is any man arrested, sued, bound over to keep the peace?

IF a woman steals from her employer, does her father, husband, brother or son serve out her term in prison?

IF a woman kills somebody, what man represents her in the prisoner's dock during her trial? What man represents her in the electric chair if she is convicted?

IF a widow or an unmarried woman fails to pay her taxes, is the property of a male relative or of the man next door sold to satisfy the debt to the State?

IF a woman forges a check, does her father, her husband, her employer, go to jail for felony?

WHY is it that the only place in the world where man wants to represent woman is at the ballot box?

? ? ?

Vote and work for the Suffrage Amendment May 24th

TEXAS EQUAL SUFFRAGE ASSOCIATION

Until 1918, every Texas adult who paid a poll tax could vote except "paupers, lunatics, felons, soldiers, sailors, and women."

Rebecca Henry Hayes of Galveston founded the state's first suffrage organization, the Texas Equal Rights Association, in 1893.

Dallas News, November 18, 1894

"The Equal Suffrage Club will appear before the next Texas legislature with a petition a mile or thereabouts long . . . asking . . . for the franchisement of women, who are tired of having no higher mission than making dumplings."

Rebecca Henry Hayes

Rebecca Hayes founded the Texas Equal Rights Association in 1893, the state's first organization for women's suffrage. Hayes was already a vice-president of the National American Woman Suffrage Association, having been appointed by Susan B. Anthony, with whom Hayes had worked as a girl in Rochester, New York. The TERA met in the Windsor Hotel in Dallas and signed up forty-eight charter members, including nine men. It was organized as an affiliate of the NAWSA, and its objective was "to advance the industrial, educational, and legal rights of women and to secure suffrage to them by appropriate state legislation." The TERA lasted until 1895.

Fifty Years to Get the Vote

It took over fifty years of hard work and three different organizations for Texas women to win the vote — from the introduction of the first resolution in 1868 until 1920 when the Nineteenth Amendment to the U. S. Constitution took effect. The Texas Legislature led the South in ratifying the Nineteenth Amendment in special session on June 23, 1919, and was the ninth state to do so.

After Rebecca Hayes's initial effort, another organization was formed by Annette Finnigan of Houston in 1903; it lasted until 1905. The final victory push (1915–1919) was led by Minnie Fisher Cunningham as president of the Texas Equal Suffrage Association.

In 1918, women achieved the right to vote in the Texas Democratic Primary. Within the seventeen-day registration period, 386,000 women signed up to vote.

The major foe of the suffrage movement was the brewery industry. There was even a Texas branch of the National Association Opposed to Woman Suffrage, organized in 1915 by Mrs. James Wells of Brownsville.

The ultimate success of the suffragists was due to sophisticated organizing, including a press campaign, grass roots county-by-county canvassing, mass meetings, petitions, leaflets, suffrage schools, and booths at the State Fair. Participation by suffragists in World War I Liberty Bond and Red Cross activities also helped swing public sentiment in their favor.

Minnie Fisher Cunningham (1882–1964) as president of the Texas Woman's Suffrage Association (1915–1919) led the final victorious fight to win the vote.

Jessie Daniel Ames (1883–1972) of Georgetown was a suffrage leader, first president of the Texas League of Women Voters, and founder of the Association of Southern Women for the Prevention of Lynching.

Minnie Fisher Cunningham and Jessie Daniel Ames cut their political teeth in the fight for women's suffrage. After that success, the two women provided leadership in a broad range of reform activities on the state and national levels.

Minnie Fisher Cunningham

The first Texas woman to get a pharmacy degree (1901), Minnie Fisher Cunningham chose politics over prescriptions and spent most of her life in the public arena. She spearheaded the final victorious push for the vote as president of the Texas Equal Suffrage Association. Cunningham may have "looked like a wren [but] she behaved like a hawk," remembered her friend Liz Carpenter.

Cunningham's competence as a Texas suffrage leader impressed the officers of the National American Woman Suffrage Association. They invited her to become the secretary of their Congressional Committee, and from 1918 to 1920 she divided her time between Austin and Washington, D. C. She is the only Texan on the suffrage plaque in the national capitol.

After suffrage became a reality in 1920, Cunningham served as executive secretary of the League of Women Voters, and then manager of the Women's National Democratic Club.

She returned to Texas to make an unsuccessful race for the U. S. Senate in 1928 (the first woman ever to run). From 1928 to 1939 she worked for the Texas A&M Agricultural Extension Service and from 1939 to 1943, for the Women's Division of the Agricultural Adjustment Administration. Defeated in a 1944 gubernatorial race, Cunningham was active

the rest of her life in the liberal wing of the Democratic Party. She and her friend Jane Y. McCallum formed the Women's Committee for Educational Freedom, and Cunningham was instrumental in the founding of the weekly, *The Texas Observer*.

Jessie Daniel Ames

"The Ku Klux Klan is alone the issue." Jessie Daniel Ames, a former suffragist, stumped the state in 1925, campaigning for gubernatorial candidate Miriam A. (Ma) Ferguson and against Ferguson's Klan-backed opponent. Not all suffragists supported (Ma) because her husband, former Governor Jim Ferguson, had been their implacable foe.

Ames's experience as a suffrage leader stood her in good stead for the next twenty years. She was the first president of the Texas League of Women Voters, a 1920 delegate to the Democratic National Convention, and organizer of the Texas branch of the American Association of University Women (AAUW).

A Methodist, she used her connections with the missionary societies to act as field representative for the Women's Committee of the Commission on Interracial Cooperation for the entire South in 1929. In 1930, Ames moved to Atlanta to organize the Association of Southern Women for the Prevention of Lynching, and she served until the South recorded its first lynchless year (1940). The association had a membership of 40,000 Southern women, backed by two million members of social, civic, and religious groups. Black women's organizations had been active against lynching for decades.

114

We were the best politicians of our day.
— Minnie Fisher Cunningham
To Jane Y. McCallum

In 1915, Baylor University women in Waco organized a suffrage club and "beat the drum" in campus parades.

Waco suffragists marched with their daughters in Votes for Women parades.

If we don't stand for something, we will fall for anything.
— Jane Y. McCallum, *Austin American Statesman,* July 1, 1945

Jane Y. McCallum (1878–1957) of Austin was the mother of five, a journalist, public relations chair of the Texas Equal Suffrage Association, and Texas Secretary of State from 1927 to 1933.

Austin women gather at the Travis County Courthouse to register to vote in a Texas primary election for the first time in 1918. Their votes helped defeat antisuffragist Governor Jim Ferguson and elect Annie Webb Blanton State Superintendent of Public Instruction (see page 65).

Jane Y. McCallum

After women won the right to vote, Jane Y. McCallum, a former suffrage leader and journalist, organized the Women's Joint Legislative Council in 1922 to drive through a program of new legislation. This coalition of women's organizations, known as the Petticoat Lobby, included the Texas Congress of Mothers and Parent Teacher Associations, the Texas Federation of Women's Clubs, the League of Women Voters, the Woman's Christian Temperance Union, the Federation of Business and Professional Women's Clubs, and later the Texas Graduate Nurses Association. They were assigned a Senate Committee room in the State Capitol as their headquarters. The Petticoat Lobby achieved Texas participation in a federal infant and maternal health care program (the Sheppard-Towner Act), emergency appropriations for Texas schools, a survey of both the education and prison systems as a prelude to basic reform, more prohibition laws, and stronger labor laws.

One legislator called their program "the most audacious piece of Bolshevism ever permitted to clutter up this chamber." It was probably the most effective public interest lobby in Texas history; it got its entire legislative program passed during its four years of work. The women countered charges of "communism, anarchism, birth control and free love" by pointing out that Texas already accepted federal subsidies for agriculture and highways, so why not for the health of mothers and babies?

Later, as Secretary of State, McCallum recovered and restored the original document of the Texas Declaration of Independence.

Jane Y. McCallum and the Senator Have Words in the Corridor

The difficulties suffragists faced can be judged by the following reported dialogue:
Senator: You ought to get married.
McCallum: But I am married.
Senator: Then you ought to be having children.
McCallum: I have five. How many do you suggest I have?
Senator: Then you should be home taking care of them.
McCallum: They're in school and their grandmother is there.
Senator: Then you should be home darning stockings.
But Jane Y. McCallum and the suffragists had the last word. Most of them were wives and mothers, and they worked long hours, days, and years for the vote. They were ultimately successful.

116

When Christia Adair was a young woman, she lived in Kingsville and worked for women's suffrage, despite the fact that the Texas Equal Suffrage Association had no black members. She continued her civil rights efforts into the 1950s and 1960s as a Houston NAACP leader and saw to it that "whites only" signs came down at the airport and public libraries.

Adair also decided it was time black department store customers were treated with respect. She selected an expensive girdle (she was very thin) and insisted on trying it on. After the manager was called, she was finally shown to a dressing room. "I bought a $27.50 girdle which I did *not* need to establish the right of Negro women to try on garments," she said.

Christia Adair (1893–) (shown here in 1920) worked for women's suffrage despite the exclusion of black women from the Texas Equal Suffrage Association.

Mrs. L. P. Evans of San Antonio casts a ballot in the November 1924 general election.

Mary Gaskey was one of many El Pasoans who cared for the wounded during the Mexican Revolution.

PASTEURIZED MILK AND CREAM
Twelve Wagons to Make Deliveries to
All Parts of the City.
Creamery Dairy Co. Phones 871

SAN ANTONIO LIGHT
AND GAZETTE

VELVET ICE CREAM
"Tastes Like More."
At fountains. Orders for banquets, re-
ceptions, lodges, club affairs or
Trade a specialty.
Creamery Dairy Co. Phones 871

VOLUME 29, No. 211   10 PAGES   SAN ANTONIO, TEXAS, WEDNESDAY, AUGUST 18, 1909   10 PAGES   PRICE: FIVE CENTS

Many women along the Texas–Mexico border were caught up in the events of the Mexican Revolution. A number, like Sara Estela Ramirez (1881–1910) who moved from Saltillo to Laredo in 1898, supported the Partido Liberál Mexicanista, a group of exiled Mexican revolutionaries who favored the emancipation of women.

"Surge! You Queen of the World"

Sara Estela Ramirez was a poet and political philosopher whose works in Spanish were widely read on both sides of the Texas–Mexico border. She lived in Laredo where she sheltered Mexican revolutionaries, made speeches, taught, and organized workers and women.

Her poem "Surge" urges women "to life, to liveliness, to the beauty of truly living" and addresses them as "queen of the world" and "goddess of universal adoration." When she died at the age of twenty-nine, she was praised as "the most illustrious Mexican woman of Texas."

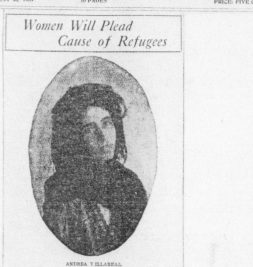

Women Will Plead Cause of Refugees

ANDREA VILLAREAL

Andrea Villareal, known as the Mexican "Joan of Arc," addressed a San Antonio rally on August 18, 1909, demanding freedom for jailed Mexican revolutionaries. She and her sister Teresa published La Mujer Moderna (The Modern Woman).

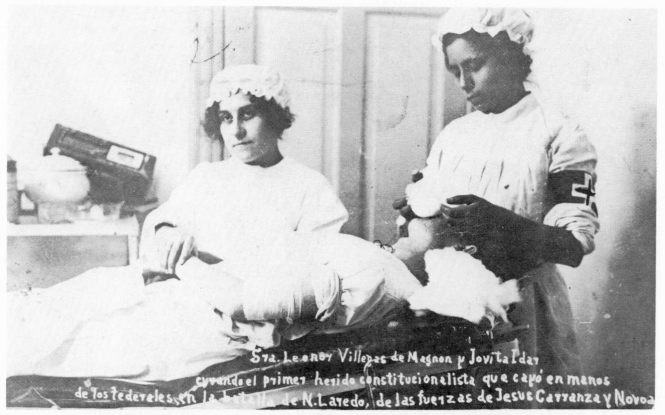

Sra. Leonor Villegas de Magnon y Jovita Idar curando el primer herido constitucionalista que cayó en manos de los federales en la batalla de N. Laredo, de las fuerzas de Jesus Carranza y Novoa

Léonor Villegas de Magnón and Jovita Idar organized La Cruz Blanca (The White Cross) on the Texas–Mexican border during the Mexican Revolution, 1913.

119

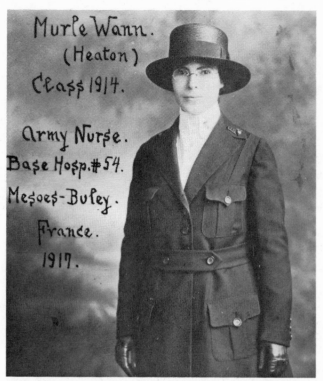

Murle Wann.
(Heaton)
Class 1914.

Army Nurse.
Base Hosp. #54.
Mesoes-Buley.
France.
1917.

Murle Wann (Heaton), a graduate of the University of Texas School of Nursing in Galveston, served as an army nurse in France in 1917.

Most Texas women supported World War I. Many went overseas as nurses or ambulance drivers. Dr. Ellen C. Cover of San Antonio went to Europe to do special medical service among the women and children of France and Belgium. Other women grew food in victory gardens, sold Liberty Bonds, rolled bandages for the Red Cross, and organized anti-vice committees around army camps.

The National Women's Party, which opposed U. S. participation in the war, had a Houston chapter, but it gained little support. After the war, it continued working on women's legal issues, such as the Equal Rights Amendment and property rights of women.

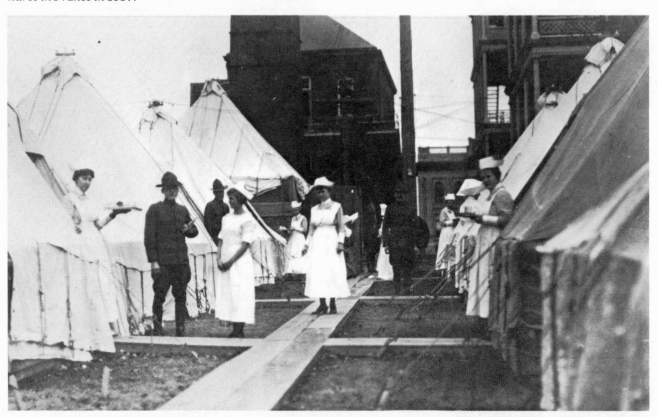

Nurses at St. Paul Hospital in Dallas set up tents on the hospital grounds to nurse refugees from the Mexican Revolution and victims of the World War I flu epidemic.

Marjorie Stinson (1896–1975) (far left) taught military flying and gunnery techniques to World War I cadets at the Stinson School of Flying in San Antonio.

At the age of seventeen, Marjorie Stinson became the youngest woman in the world to receive a pilot's license in 1914. She practiced with a plane balanced on a wooden horse.

Stinson became one of the best flight instructors in the country. In 1915 and 1916 she trained over eighty male pilots — mostly Canadian — for service in World War I.

Marjorie Stinson flew the first airmail route in Texas from San Antonio to Seguin — in 1915. She was the first woman to serve in the U. S. Aviation Reserve Corps (1915). From 1917 to 1928, she was the foremost daredevil stunt pilot in the nation. Stinson barnstormed the country, thrilling audiences at county fairs and airports with her 1500-foot plunges and upside down flying.

Later Marjorie Stinson and her brother Eddie Stinson designed successful planes for the Stinson Aircraft Corporation in Detroit. In 1930, she took a job as a draftsman for the U. S. War Department in Washington, D. C., and stayed fifteen years. After her retirement, she researched the history of aviation. After her death, her ashes were scattered over Stinson Field in San Antonio.

Helen Moore, a Texas City nurse, founded that city's first library, worked for suffrage, was president of the Texas League of Women Voters, and was one of the first women in the Texas Legislature (1929–1937).

State Senator Margie Neal served from 1927 to 1935. Neal's leadership resulted in the passage of much progressive legislation, including free tuition for public school children ages six to twenty-one, part-time evening schools, and a widow's aid law. She was the first female member of the Texas State Democratic Executive Committee.

From 1922 to 1985, forty-six women have served in the Texas Legislature, forty-one in the House and six in the Senate. One woman, Neveille Colson of Navasota, served twenty-eight years in both chambers (1939–1949 in the House, 1949–1967 in the Senate). She authored many laws in the areas of farm-to-market roads, schools, soil and water conservation, and public health.

In 1985, as a result of the civil rights and women's movements, there were fifteen female representatives, mostly Democrats (including three black and two brown women), but still only one female senator, a Republican, Cynthia Krier.

Women's political influence, however, has been felt in other ways. Political parties have depended heavily upon their volunteer work in fund raising, voter registration and turn-out, organization building, and as members of national executive and program committees.

Texas women held public office even before they were allowed to vote. In 1902, Mrs. L. P. Carlisle became the first woman office holder in Texas, appointed as Hunt County's county clerk to succeed her husband. Two women were elected to the Dallas School Board in 1908. But winning the vote was a great move forward in the area of women's legal rights. During the 1920s hundreds of women ran for and some won political office — city council, county school superintendents, even governor. By 1929, of the state's 254 county treasurers 109 were women. That first decade two were elected to the House of Representatives (Edith Wilmans of Dallas in 1922 and Helen Moore of Texas City in 1928) and one to the Senate (Margie Neal of Carthage in 1926).

Margie Neal (1875–1971) of Carthage edited the Texas Mule *in 1903, and became the first woman elected to the Texas Senate in 1926.*

122

MIRIAM A. FERGUSON
Candidate for Governor
SECOND TERM
SUBJECT TO THE ACTION OF THE DEMOCRATIC PRIMARY, JULY 24, 1926

1. Read what Ferguson-ism has done for Texas.

2. A man who will not read both sides of a question is dishonest.—Abraham Lincoln.

3. Do not send a boy to mill.

4. The State is now on a cash basis, and there is money in the Treasury.

5. The penitentiary is paying its way.

6. Taxes have been reduced.

7. No strikes or lynchings.

8. The schools are being run economically and efficiently.

9. The insane have been taken out of jails.

10. Mercy and forgiveness is extended to the friendless and unfortunate.

11. All these a woman Governor has brought to Texas.

12. Why change?

Governor Miriam A. Wallace (Ma) Ferguson (1875–1961)

Miriam A. Ferguson, Texas's only woman governor, served two terms, 1925–1927 and 1933–1935. She was elected over the objections of most suffragists. Her husband James Ferguson had been one of the country's greatest opponents of woman suffrage, but because he was ineligible to run again for governor, having been impeached, he urged his wife to run.

During her first term, Ma got an anti-mask law aimed at the Ku Klux Klan passed, cut taxes, and issued almost 2,000 pardons and paroles, mostly in alcohol-related offenses, complaining that those laws were enforced only against the poor. She supported aid to schools and prison reform and appointed the first woman secretary of state, Emma Meharg.

Governor Ferguson's "Pay As You Go" call for a balanced budget got her reelected governor in 1932. She asked President Franklin Roosevelt to lend farmers money on cotton as a price support and took advantage of all the New Deal social welfare programs. The Texas Constitution was amended to allow $20 million in bread bonds to feed the poor. In an effort to cut state expenses, she slashed state salaries, legalized betting, eliminated the art and journalism departments from UT-Austin, and promoted a state sales tax which failed. She proposed a tax on oil and instituted state regulation of the oil industry.

Ma Ferguson was defeated in her race for a third term by W. Lee (Pappy) O'Daniel in 1940, but she remained interested in state and national politics the rest of her life and campaigned for Democratic Party candidates.

Although Mrs. Ferguson originally shared her husband's belief that a woman's place was in the home, she finally came to the conclusion that "They gave us the vote, we might as well use it."

During the Depression, San Antonio pecan shellers like María del Refugio Ozuna (left), age thirteen, and Mrs. San Juan Gonzales (right), age seventy-seven, earned six cents (and even less) an hour for a fifty-four-hour week.

The 1930s were marked by massive unemployment in Texas, accompanied by major union organizing drives among men and women.

In 1938, young Emma Tenayuca led 10,000 San Antonio pecan shellers out on strike. At that time, it was the largest labor walkout in Texas history. Most of the workers were poor Mexican-American women who sorted pecans in hot, dusty sheds, which were dimly lit and barely ventilated. They worked fifty-four hours a week for six cents an hour in San Antonio's number one industry. The local Women's International League for Peace and Freedom raised funds to feed the strikers.

The strike was long and bitter; the workers won a temporary victory, but the growers eventually turned to machines for shelling. Tenayuca recalled, "What had once been a struggle for jobs had become a mass movement for jobs, against deportation, against discrimination, for justice." Emma Tenayuca is still regarded as a folk heroine by those who remember her fiery leadership and staunch courage in the face of official harassment and hostility.

Emma Tenayuca, with hat and paper, organized San Antonio workers. She is shown here at the Federal Building protesting alleged beatings of Mexican-Americans, including Enrique Perez (third from left) by the Border Patrol, 1937.

Employees of the Finck Cigar Factory, San Antonio, picket the plant wearing banners reading,
WE ARE STRIKING FOR BETTER CONDITIONS, *1933.*

SOME WOMEN EARNED TWO CENTS AN HOUR

During the Depression the garment industry relied on parceling out piece goods to be sewn by women of many ethnic groups in their homes on a contract basis.

In 1932, investigators for the U. S. Women's Bureau found Hispanic women in San Antonio working as many as ten to fifteen hours a day for as little as two to five cents an hour.

Five years later, Myrle Zappone, a leader of the International Ladies Garment Workers Union (ILGWU), organized a successful strike which resulted in a wage increase and fewer hours.

Skilled seamstresses worked at home for starvation wages during the Depression.

Charlotte Graham (1912–) (left) led a strike of the International Ladies Garment Workers Union (ILGWU) in 1935 against thirteen Dallas clothing manufacturers.

Charlotte Graham described the garment factory in which she worked as a hot and dirty place with no fans, where lint and dust hung from the ceiling. She said management cared more for the machines than for the workers.

Once when Graham ran a needle through her finger, breaking it off inside, she waited an hour and a half for a doctor. She received no time off or compensation. Workers could use the bathroom only during lunch and a 15-minute break. Conditions improved somewhat after the adoption of codes by the New Deal's National Recovery Administration (1933–1935).

Graham and other ILGWU leaders were blacklisted in Dallas after they led the strike. Later, federal legislation made it illegal to blacklist union organizers. Graham was eventually rehired by her former employer.

Juanita Craft (1902–1985), organizer of 182 branches of the NAACP, is shown with state and national leaders, ca. 1940s. (Back row, far right is NAACP counsel Thurgood Marshall, who was later appointed an Associate Justice, U. S. Supreme Court, in 1967. Front row, second from right, is Walter White, longtime national NAACP secretary.)

From the 1940s through the 1960s, NAACP leaders like Juanita Craft and Christia Adair organized campaigns in Dallas and Houston to end violence against blacks and to integrate public facilities, such as libraries, airports, restaurants, and department stores. Many white men and women supported their efforts.

Juanita Craft

Juanita Craft organized 182 Texas chapters of the National Association for the Advancement of Colored People (NAACP). She registered voters, formed youth groups, headed get-out-the-vote drives, worked to end legal discrimination, and served on the Dallas City Council.

Hispanic Women and Civil Rights

Mexican-American women have a long history of civil rights activity. Maria Hernandez (pictured at right) is only one of a long line of Hispanic women who have been active in the fight for justice and equal opportunities.

During the 1940s and 1950s, Hispanic women turned from the activism of the labor movement to organizations such as LULAC (League of United Latin American Citizens) and the American GI Forum, where they worked on education, voter registration, and jobs.

One of the most influential Hispanic women in the U. S. is Vilma Martinez of San Antonio, the first to serve as chair of the University of California Board of Regents. Martinez was formerly head of the Mexican American Legal Defense and Education Fund (MALDEF) and played a key role in the passage of the Voting Rights Act of 1965. She wrote the brief for the first equal employment case tried under the 1964 Civil Rights Act before the U. S. Supreme Court.

In the 1960s and 1970s, Mexican-American women sought political office. Virginia Musquíz was the first to run for the state legislature in 1964, under the banner of a new political party, La Raza Unida, of which she was a founder. She lost, but ten years later Irma Rangel of Kingsville became the first Hispanic woman elected to the Texas Legislature. In 1984, Lena Guerrero became the second. Hispanic women were active in the women's movement of the 1970s but formed their own caucuses within such organizations as the Texas Women's Political Caucus.

Maria Hernandez of Lytle and her husband organized a civic and civil rights organization in 1929. She has been active for over forty years in fighting for desegregation and justice for her people.

128

7

WAR, POLITICS, AND PEACE

When World War II broke out, Texas women threw their support behind that effort. They joined the armed services and the WASPS and many took jobs in war industries. World War II, like World War I, created nontraditional economic opportunities for women, and wages in traditional jobs like domestic work rose.

After the war, many women continued working. Others stayed active in civil rights, clubs, and nonpartisan organizations. Women finally won the right to serve on juries in 1954, due largely to the work of the League of Women Voters. Other women worked in the Republican Party, the Democratic Party, and La Raza Unida, a new Hispanic political party. With fifty-one percent of Texas women over the age of sixteen in the labor force by 1978, the labor movement became increasingly important.

The women's movement of the 1960s and 1970s drew a broad spectrum of Texas women into activism and gave a boost to the continuing efforts of older organizations. The Texas Business and Professional Women's Clubs, which had been trying for twenty-five years to get an Equal Legal Rights Amendment to the Texas Constitution, at last achieved that goal in 1972. The Texas Women's Political Caucus was formed and began to work at getting women in political office. Partly through their efforts, a new wave of office holders, both elective and appointive, appeared. Texas women organized at state and national levels both for and against a federal Equal Rights Amendment and abortion law reform. An Austin attorney, Sarah Ragle Weddington, in *Roe v. Wade* (1973) was successful in establishing the right to abortion for women all over the country.

Women's centers, battered women's shelters, rape crisis centers, and women's arts organizations were founded. Women still fought for issues of importance to children — improved child care, textbook reform, and bilingual education, for example — and were leaders in the peace, antinuclear, and environmental movements. Women's sports at the university level gained funding and visibility; and university women won (and sometimes lost) hard-fought battles for equal pay, equal promotions, and tenure. Women's studies programs were instituted at many Texas colleges and universities.

In 1981, a statewide exhibition, sponsored by the Texas Foundation for Women's Resources, opened. Known as "Texas Women, A Celebration of History," it toured the state for two years and ended a long silence about women's contributions to the state.

Although women were entering nontraditional occupations and professions in larger numbers and more were graduating from universities, as of 1985 there was still much to be done. Women still earned only sixty-three cents for every dollar earned by men, and most were still segregated in lower-paying occupations.

With the acceleration of the arms race, women in 1985 became increasingly active on behalf of world peace, and many Texans attended the International Women's Conference in Nairobi, Kenya.

Miss Placencia of San Antonio was the first Mexican-American woman to be commissioned as a navy nurse in World War II.

Military Service

World War II marked the first major military involvement of Texas women in a war effort. Women served in the WACS, WAVES, and WASPS.

Sweetwater, Texas, was the site of the only all-woman air base in history, Avenger Field. Over 25,000 women applied for jobs with the Women's Airforce Service Pilots (WASPS), but only 1,074 passed all the tests. Famed aviator Jacqueline Cochran was their leader.

WASPS ferried war planes; towed targets for live gunnery practice; trained pilots, navigators and bombardiers; and tested new and newly repaired aircraft. They ran simulated strafing and smoke-laying missions. They flew sixty million miles.

Thirty-eight WASPS lost their lives serving their country without military benefits or rank but subject to military discipline. Finally in 1979, thirty-four years after the war ended, surviving WASPS were granted retirement benefits by Congress.

Lila Cockrell, later a three-term mayor of San Antonio, was commanding officer of a company of WAVES judged "best commanded and performed" in the Bureau of Ships. Edna Gardner Whyte, who had received her pilot's license in 1926, trained Army and Navy pilots in the early stages of World War II.

Over 1,000 WASPS (Women's Airforce Service Pilots) formed the first group of women pilots ever trained and deployed in a military effort at Avenger Field Air Base in Sweetwater from 1942 to 1944.

The Home Front

Many more women served on the home front, filling jobs vacated by servicemen in plants converted from peacetime to wartime manufacturing. Women also served as air raid wardens, rollers of bandages, collectors of scrap metal, and sellers of war bonds. The war effort broke down sex barriers in some traditionally male occupations.

Colonel Oveta Culp Hobby (1905–) of Houston was the first woman to receive the Distinguished Service Cross, earned as the first director of the Women's Army Corps (WACS) in World War II.

Colonel Oveta Culp Hobby helped break numerous barriers for women in the military. She led more than 100,000 women in the war effort.

Oveta Culp Hobby

Oveta Culp Hobby was the first director of the Women's Army Corps (WACS) formed after Pearl Harbor and the U. S. entry into World War II. Hobby led more than 100,000 women in the war effort, including 8,000 from Texas.

In 1953, Hobby was appointed by President Dwight Eisenhower as his first Secretary of Health, Education, and Welfare. She later became publisher of the *Houston Post*. She was married to former governor Will Hobby from 1931 to 1964; her son is Texas Lieutenant Governor William P. (Bill) Hobby.

Frankie Randolph (1894 – 1972) was president of the Houston Junior League in the 1920s; founder of the liberal paper, the Texas Observer, *in 1954; a state Democratic Party leader; and was elected to the National Democratic Committee in 1956.*

Even after World War II and their involvement in the war effort, women still had not achieved full political rights. They returned to homemaking in large numbers and continued their activities in public life through clubs, civic organizations, and political parties. The League of Women Voters concentrated on international issues, voter registration, and abolishing the poll tax. Largely through the League's efforts and those of the Texas Business & Professional Women's Clubs, women finally got the right to serve on Texas juries in 1954. That year the U. S. Supreme Court issued its *Brown* v. *Board of Education* decision, mandating the desegregation of public schools, but the decision was slow to be implemented.

Women's participation in the Democratic and Republican parties increased during these decades, but their representation in the legislature was still quite small. The election of John Tower to the U. S. Senate on the Republican ticket helped move Texas toward two-party status. But being a Republican in some counties was still unpopular. Shirley Ratisseau Dimmick of Aransas County, the first female GOP chair, was forced to hold the 1962 Republican primary under an oak tree in her front yard when no public facility was available. She awoke on election morning to find five dead rattlesnakes tied to her fence post and a sign reading, "No two-party."

Women were active in other groups as well. In 1953 Judge Sarah T. Hughes became the Dallas United Nations Association's first chair and led it through a period of attacks by that city's conservatives. In Houston Minute Women packed a meeting of the local school board in 1953, objecting to textbooks which they considered un-American. And Austinite Madalyn Murray O'Hair was the principal in a successful case before the U. S. Supreme Court which removed Bible readings and recitation of the Lord's Prayer from public schools (*Murray et al.* v. *Curlett et al.*, 1963).

Mrs. Charles B. White was the first black Texan elected to public office since Reconstruction. She served on the Houston School Board from 1958 to 1967.

Many Mexican-American women and children have worked in Texas fields producing food under difficult conditions. Under the leadership of Rebecca Flores Harrington, director of the Texas United Farm Workers of America (AFL-CIO), farm workers in the 1980s have made important gains, including workers' compensation, unemployment benefits, pesticide regulations, and toilets in the field.

133

The Honorable Anne Armstrong (1927–) served as U.S. Ambassador to the British Court of St. James's from 1976 to 1977. She was a counselor with cabinet rank to Presidents Richard Nixon and Gerald Ford.

Presidential appointments of Texas women occurred in the 1960s and 1970s. President Dwight D. Eisenhower appointed Dr. Zelma George as a member of the U. S. delegation to the United Nations Fifteenth General Assembly. President Gerald Ford appointed Anne Armstrong as the first woman ever to be U. S. Ambassador to the Court of St. James's (Great Britain), and President Jimmy Carter appointed Dr. Blandina Cárdenas Ramirez to the U.S. Civil Rights Commission.

Anne Legendre (Mrs. Tobin) Armstrong

Anne Armstrong has been an important national leader in the Republican Party for over twenty years. She was the first woman in the history of either major party to be a keynote speaker when she addressed the 1972 Republican National Convention. That year she became cochair of the Republican National Committee and a counselor with cabinet rank to President Richard M. Nixon. Armstrong was instrumental in creating Nixon's Office of Women's Programs and was an early supporter of the Equal Rights Amendment. She was a key figure in the administration of President Ford as well. In 1985, Armstrong organized a nonpartisan group, the Texas Women's Alliance, for those with moderate to conservative political views.

Dr. Zelma George

Dr. Zelma George has had a distinguished career as an opera singer, diplomat, and social worker.

She played starring roles in two of Gian-Carlo Menotti's operas, *The Medium* and *The Consul*. She was a U. S. delegate to the United Nations in 1960, head of the Cleveland Job Corps for Women in the 1970s, and in 1982 marched against nuclear armaments in her motorized wheelchair.

Dr. Zelma George (1904–), a distinguished diplomat and member of the U. S. delegation to the Fifteenth General Assembly of the United Nations in 1960, won the Dag Hammerskjold Award for Contributions to International Understanding.

Liz Carpenter (1920–) of Austin has been a journalist; assistant to Vice-President Lyndon B. Johnson; an Assistant Secretary of Public Affairs, U. S. Department of Education; and national chair of ERAmerica.

Liz Carpenter

Liz (Sutherland) Carpenter, a fifth-generation Texan, covered Congress and the White House as a journalist and has been a high-level government spokesperson. She and her husband founded a news bureau, and in 1954 she was president of the Women's National Press Club. She was executive assistant to Vice-President Lyndon Johnson (1960–1963). When he became president, Carpenter was press secretary and staff director to Lady Bird Johnson (1963–1968).

Carpenter described her White House experiences in the best-seller *Ruffles and Flourishes*.

A founder of the National Women's Political Caucus in 1971, Liz Carpenter was chair of ERAmerica, a national organization supporting the Equal Rights Amendment to the U. S. Constitution. She was also Assistant Secretary of Public Affairs in the U. S. Department of Education from 1979 to 1980.

135

Many new organizations and agencies sprang up in the wake of the 1970s women's movement. The nonpartisan National Women's Political Caucus was founded in 1971. Its first chair was a Texas attorney, Frances (Sissy) Farenthold (see page 139). Organizations like the National Organization for Women (NOW) and the Women's Equity Action League (WEAL) began to work on issues such as sexism in textbooks and the media, equal opportunity in employment, the Equal Rights Amendment, and changes in laws affecting women.

Women's centers, battered women's shelters, and rape crisis centers, among others, were set up in many Texas cities.

Dr. Nikki R. Van Hightower was founder and first president of the Houston Area Women's Center. It opened in 1977.

Gerry Beer was founder and first president of Dallas's Family Place, a shelter for battered women and their children, which opened in 1979.

In 1975, Texas women demonstrated in front of the state capitol in Austin, opposing efforts to rescind the 1973 vote of the Texas Legislature in favor of the national Equal Rights Amendment.

Jane Hickie, an Austin attorney, was the second chair of the Texas Women's Political Caucus in 1973. She was later an aide to Travis County Commissioner Ann Richards and Richards's campaign manager in her successful race for state treasurer in 1982.

Texas voters, by a 4-to-1 majority, approved a state Equal Legal Rights Amendment to the Texas Constitution in 1972. Prior to its passage, Texas was one of the nation's most legally discriminatory states against women, according to attorney Hermine Tobolowsky, the Mother of the Texas ERA. Medical treatment of a married woman or a child required a man's authorization, and emergency care could be denied if a man could not be contacted to grant permission. The Texas ERA rendered such discriminatory legislation void.

In 1973, the Texas Legislature became the first Southern body to ratify the national Equal Rights Amendment. Later efforts by some conservative women's groups to rescind that decision have failed.

In 1977, a major national federally sponsored women's conference, known as International Women's Year (IWY), was held in Houston to set goals for women's collective achievement. While a majority of those attending were feminists, there was an anti-feminist presence there as well.

137

Sarah Weddington (1945–) of Austin argued the case Roe v. Wade *before the U. S. Supreme Court in 1973 which legalized abortion, and was an advisor on women's issues to President Jimmy Carter (1979–1981).*

Barbara Jordan (1936–) of Houston was the first black elected to the Texas Senate and to the U. S. Congress since Reconstruction. She served in the State Senate from 1966 to 1972 and in Congress as the first black woman from the South ever, from 1973 to 1979.

Sarah Weddington at age twenty-eight gained national attention as the attorney who successfully argued the case *Roe v. Wade* before the U. S. Supreme Court in 1973. The Court rendered a landmark decision giving women a constitutional right to choose an abortion.

As a member of the Texas House of Representatives (1973–1977), Weddington advocated increased salaries for state employees, public kindergartens, improved health care, reform of the rape statutes, and passage of the Equal Rights Amendment. From 1977 to 1979, Weddington was general counsel to the U. S. Department of Agriculture; from 1979 to 1981, advisor to President Jimmy Carter on women's issues; and later one of his senior advisors. She headed Texas's Office of State-Federal Relations in Washington, D. C., from 1983 to 1985.

Barbara Jordan

When Barbara Jordan was elected to the Texas Senate in 1966, she became the first black of that chamber in the twentieth century. She went on to a distinguished career in the U. S. Congress. As a member of the House Judiciary Committee, she achieved fame for an eloquent speech during the hearings considering impeachment of then-President Richard Nixon:

'We, the People'—it is a very eloquent beginning. But when the Constitution of the United States was completed on the 17th of September in 1787, I was not included in that 'We, the People.' I felt for many years that somehow George Washington and Alexander Hamilton just left me out by mistake. But through the process of amendment, interpretation and court decision I have finally been included in 'We, the People.' (July 25, 1974)

Since retiring from Congress, Jordan has been a professor at the Lyndon B. Johnson School of Public Affairs, UT-Austin.

Texas has had only one other female representative in Congress. In 1966, Mrs. Lera Thomas of Houston was appointed to complete the term of her deceased husband Albert.

Frances Tarlton (Sissy) Farenthold

In 1972, Frances Farenthold became the first woman in U. S. history nominated for Vice-President and voted upon at the Democratic National Convention. (Sarah T. Hughes of Dallas was nominated in 1952 but withdrew her name.) From 1969 to 1973, Farenthold was the only woman in the Texas House. (Barbara Jordan was the only female state senator at the time.) As a member of the House Committee on State Affairs, Farenthold was instrumental in the 1972 passage of the Texas Equal Legal Rights Amendment — a law for which women, especially the Business and Professional Women's Clubs, had been lobbying for twenty-five years.

Farenthold led a group of "Dirty Thirty" reform legislators who opposed the Speaker of the Texas House in the Sharpstown scandal involving stock manipulations. As a Texas gubernatorial candidate in the Democratic Party primary in 1972, Farenthold ran second in a field of seven, forcing Dolph Briscoe into a runoff. She garnered 884,000 votes even though she was defeated. She ran for governor again in 1974 but was defeated. She was the first female president of Wells College in New York (1976–1979) and later returned to Texas in the 1980s to practice law in Houston.

"THAT LADY" FOR GOVERNOR FARENTHOLD

"REFORM CONSISTS OF HONEST MEN AND WOMEN SERVING IN OFFICE, PEOPLE WHO DO NOT ENRICH THEMSELVES WHILE HOLDING PUBLIC OFFICE BY MERGING THE PUBLIC WITH PRIVATE INTEREST . . ."

Martha Cotera (1947–) of Austin was a candidate for the State Board of Education in 1972 on the ticket of a new party, La Raza Unida.

139

With the growth of the women's movement, the number of female legislators began to increase in 1973. By the 1985-1987 session, there were fifteen women serving, an all-time high (see pages 122, 162).

State Representative Wilhelmina Fitzgerald Delco of Austin was in 1985 the only woman to head a Texas House of Representatives Committee — the Higher Education Committee. She was elected in 1974, the first black from Travis County, and has been a champion of funding equity for black state colleges.

State Representative Irma Rangel of Kingsville, an attorney, was the first Hispanic woman elected to the Texas House of Representatives in 1976; she has been reelected four times.

State Representative Lena Guerrero, also an attorney, was elected in 1984 to represent Travis County. She was formerly president of the Texas Women's Political Caucus.

Newly elected Republican State Senator Cyndi Taylor Krier of San Antonio was refused entrance to the floor for the opening of the legislature January 16, 1985, because two doorkeepers failed to recognize her. A fellow senator gave her a giant badge for future identification.

Emma Long was Austin's first female city council member; she served two terms (1948–1959, 1963–1969).

During the 1970s and 1980s, four of Texas's largest cities have had female mayors. The first was Lila Cockrell, a three-term mayor of San Antonio (1975–1981); the second was Dallas's Adlene Harrison, who served as interim mayor in 1976. In 1977, Austin elected Carole Keeton (then McClellan) Rylander who served three terms, and in 1981, Houston elected Kathy Whitmire. Whitmire was reelected in 1983 and 1985. Dallas has also had two mayors pro tem, Adlene Harrison and Annette Strauss.

Many women have also served on city councils during these years. Anita Martinez of Dallas became the first Hispanic woman to serve on a city council upon her election in 1969. It was another twelve years before the second Hispanic woman was elected — Maria Berriozabal of San Antonio in 1981.

Carole Keeton [McClellan] Rylander was elected Austin's first woman mayor in 1977 and served three terms. In 1983, she became the first woman appointed to the State Board of Insurance.

Mayor Kathy Whitmire (1946–) was elected Houston's first woman comptroller in 1977 and its first woman mayor in 1981. She was reelected in 1983 and 1985.

Secretary of State Myra McDaniel (1933–) made history as the first black ever to call a Texas House of Representatives opening session to order (January 15, 1985). In 1984, McDaniel, an attorney appointed by Governor Mark White, became the third female Secretary of State. The other two were Emma Meharg (1925-1927) and Jane Y. McCallum (1927–1933).

Myra (Atwell) McDaniel made history when she was appointed Texas Secretary of State in 1984 by Governor Mark White. She became the state's chief elections officer and was responsible for voter registration. In this position she became the holder of the highest political office of any black in Texas; she is also the first black and the third woman to hold that office.

McDaniel has had a distinguished career in government and the private sector. She was the first woman to serve as chief legal counsel to a Texas governor (1983–1984).

State Treasurer Ann Willis Richards (1933–) addresses a joint session of the Texas Legislature on June 12, 1984, to present solutions to the state's cash flow problems. She is shown here shaking hands with Lieutenant Governor Bill Hobby.

Ann Richards was the first Texas woman in fifty years to win statewide office in 1982 when she was elected State Treasurer. She became the first women ever to hold that office. Richards received 1,883,781 votes, beating her opponent by almost 2-to-1; and she carried all but thirteen of the state's 254 counties.

Only two other women have ever held statewide elective office — Dr. Annie Webb Blanton, State Superintendent of Public Instruction, from 1919 to 1923 (see page 65), and Governor Miriam A. (Ma) Ferguson, from 1925 to 1927 and from 1933 to 1935 (see page 123).

In her first three years of office, Richards turned the Treasury into a model state agency and financial institution sparkling with efficiency and effectiveness. Richards earned taxpayers an additional $100 million more than would have been possible under the practices of her predecessor. She automated the processing of funds so that no check stays in the Treasury longer than ninety minutes. She instituted rapid deposit programs to reduce time lags and costs associated with collections and deposits of other state agencies. She stepped up the hiring and promotion

of minorities and women under an aggressive affirmative action policy. *Texas Business* featured her on the cover of their September 1983, issue, giving her an A in innovation. They said, "With more public officials like Richards, Texas would have one of the best governments people could rightfully hope for."

Richards had previously served as a Travis County Commissioner (1976–1982) and as a member of President Jimmy Carter's Advisory Committee for Women. She has been a longtime advocate of women's rights and honored by the National Women's Political Caucus, among other groups.

Twelve women were inducted into the first Texas Women's Hall of Fame in September, 1984.

The Governor's Commission for Women inaugurated a Texas Women's Hall of Fame on September 13, 1984, with the induction of twelve living women honored in ten areas of achievement. Left to right seated:

      Christia Adair, Civic and Volunteer Involvement

      Dr. Amy Freeman Lee, Arts and Humanities

      Vivian Castleberry, Communication

      Dr. Kate Atkinson Bell, Education

      Dr. Clotilde Garcia, Health Professions

      Barbara Jordan, Public Service.

Left to right standing:

      Lila Cockrell, Community Leadership

      Governor Mark White

      Dr. Mary Evelyn Blagg Huey, Education

      Dr. Jeane Porter Hester, Science and Technology

      Lady Bird Johnson, Public Service

Not pictured are Judge Sarah T. Hughes, Legal, and Oveta Culp Hobby, Business and Finance.

In 1985, 200 women were nominated, and twelve were selected. They included Ann Richards, Public Service; Liz Carpenter, Communications; Maria Elena Flood, Education; Grace Woodruff Cartwright, Agriculture and Ranching; Jenny Lind Porter, Literary Arts; Lydia Mendoza, Performing Arts; Edna Gardner Whyte, Business and Finance; Willie Lee Glass, Civic Leadership; Dr. Benjy Frances Brooks, Health Professions; Louise B. Raggio, Legal; Patricia Happ Buffler, Science and Technology; and Helen Farabee, Volunteerism.

The internationally known artist Georgia O'Keefe, who taught art at Texas State Normal College in Canyon from 1916 to 1918, was forced from her job because of her opposition to World War I. But most Texas women (and men) supported U. S. participation.

After the end of hostilities, the Texas Federation of Women's Clubs celebrated "No More War" days and backed U. S. entry into the League of Nations. They sponsored programs on disarmament and international relations. Anna Pennybacker, the great Federation of Women's Clubs leader, toured as a speaker on behalf of disarmament and was a foreign correspondent at the League of Nations in Geneva for three newspapers.

Ima Hogg, the Houston philanthropist, said, "In a world struggling toward peace and a universal humanitarian regard for mankind, there is no place for an aloof or exclusive institution." The activities of the Pan American Round Table, which had been organized before the war by Florence Terry Griswold of San Antonio, envisioned a union of women of the Americas which would bring about a permanent peace.

Is there no cure for the madness of war? . . . Must unoffending youth forever pay for the crime of those who breed and foment war? . . . What are we women going to do about it? . . . We can teach the children in the schools that war is a crime. . . . 'That it is greater to be a soldier of peace than a soldier of war . . . .' We women . . . can demand the outlawry of war. . . . The world is watching us.
—*Mrs. Lee Joseph, President, Texas Federation of Women's Clubs, 1919, "World Peace"*

Mary Catherine McCabe rides on the Marfa History Club float in the World Peace Parade, ca. 1930s.

After World War II, women again took up the cause of peace and disarmament. They were active in supporting the formation of the United Nations, the adoption of the Universal Declaration of Human Rights, and the creation of the specialized agencies, particularly those affecting the welfare of women and children. The League of Women Voters began studying a whole host of international issues as a major part of its program agenda.

Cordye Hall, a Dallas peace activist, explained the reasons for her involvement in trying to prevent another war:

I didn't want something to happen to the young people. The major factor that probably accounted for my unusual activity in pursuit of peace was when I saw my oldest brother completely disabled in World War I. I gradually became disillusioned. 'Make the world safe for democracy?' It didn't. I couldn't object to World War II as I did to the first World War because Hitler had to be stopped. But I thought about how I'd spent my whole youth raising my two kids to adulthood. The older one was just out of high school and had to go into a war with all its harrowing experiences. We lost so many of my son's friends. . . . Many didn't come back. I used to sit by the radio for hours following the war very closely, and when it was over, I began anew to find a substitute for war.

Mrs. Hall joined with Judge Sarah T. Hughes and other Dallasites to organize first the World Federalists and then the Dallas United Nations Association. She believed in world peace through international law to take the place of nations shooting it out.

Austin women made a United Nations quilt after World War II.

Cordye Hall (1899–) has been active for world peace for over forty years. After World War II, she helped found the Dallas United Nations Association. During the Vietnam War, she picketed as a member of Another Mother for Peace and in 1979, at the age of eighty demonstrated against a nuclear power plant in North Texas.

147

In 1985, Texas women reached out to their neighbors in Mexico and participated in an international conference in Africa.

Women and World Issues, an Austin organization, sponsored a binational workshop, "Women and Food Production: A Texas-Mexico Dialogue," at UT-Austin. Over 250 farm workers, educators, nurses, nutritionists, religious leaders, and businesswomen gathered to discuss common concerns and experiences.

And a number of Texans traveled to Nairobi, Kenya, in July for the United Nations End of the Decade Conference. Beryl Milburn of Austin, a member of UT-Austin's Board of Regents, was a member of the official U. S. delegation. Other Texans participated in the Forum '85 activities, consisting of representatives of nongovernment organizations. They included Frances Farenthold of Houston, who assisted in running the Peace Tent, and Idelle Rabin of Dallas, a national vice-president of the American Jewish Committee.

Idelle Rabin, Dallas businesswoman, and Njeri Mungai, Kenya's largest string bean farmer who employs 200 women, at the International Women's Conference, Nairobi, July, 1985.

Dr. Dorothea W. Brown, president, Austin Chapter of LINKS, INC., welcomes Dr. Guillermina Valdéz of Juarez, Mexico, at a conference on "Women in Food Production: A Texas–Mexico Dialogue."

8

A CELEBRATION OF LIFE

Growing up, going to school, being a teenager, a single woman, a bride, a mother, an aunt, a grandmother, and often a widow . . . the lives of Texas women are woven together with the lives of their families and friends.

For many stages of growth, there are rituals and celebrations. Here are photographs that capture some personal moments in history.

Suey Gee Eng and Yuck Lon Leung (left to right), at the opening of the San Antonio Chinese School, 1928.

Martha Lathan Pierce, Center, Texas

Maria and Mersedes Cabazos (?), San Antonio, 1916.

Martha Frances Winegarten, [now Wilson] Dallas, 1956.

Texas Woman's University basketball team, in the 1920s.

Stuart Female Academy students, Austin, on an outing to Mt. Bonnell, ca. 1900.

Girls will be girls.

L. C. Anderson High School students choose a queen.

Emily Burken, Independent Choreographers Alliance, performs for Women and Their Work.

Three ladies clowning.

Celia (Cohen) Lewin, Dallas, 1926.

The wedding party of Hattie Campbell, Ebenezer Baptist Church, Austin, 1909.

Mrs. Lucía Garcia de Guerrero, San Antonio, mother of five children.

Wichita women and baby.

A Dallas family. Parents seated are Max and Jenny Cohen. Their daughters (left to right, front row) Rosa, Doris, Esther, and (standing) Celia.

Women's Progressive Club, San Antonio.

St. Vincent de Paul nurses at St. Paul Hospital, Dallas, in the 1960s.

Rosa von Roeder Kleberg and her family.

The Reverend Lynn (Sweeney) Stipulkosky (Rockport and Austin), whose Gunderman, Ratisseau, and Sweeney ancestors were 1830s Texas pioneers. A Texan and mother, she was ordained a Methodist minister in 1985.

Cecilia Rucker Collins, president of the Travis County Home Demonstration Club, 1945–1946.

Rosa Granillo bakes bread in an outdoor oven, 1960.

Lydia Mendoza of Houston, singer and guitarist of Norteño music and National Endowment for the Arts award winner.

Ginger Rogers performs at the opening of the "Texas Women, A Celebration of History" exhibit, San Antonio, May 1981.

WOMEN WHO HAVE SERVED IN THE TEXAS LEGISLATURE

Through December 31, 1985

Senate

Margie Neal Carthage	1927–1935	Frances Farenthold Corpus Christi	1969–1973
Mrs. Lacy Stewart Houston	1947–1949	Kay Bailey Houston	1973–1977
Neveille Colson Navasota	1949–1967	Eddie Bernice Johnson Dallas	1973–1979
Barbara Jordan Houston	1967–1973	Chris Miller Fort Worth	1973–1979
Betty Andujar Fort Worth	1973–1983	Senfronia Thompson Houston	1973–
Cynthia Taylor Krier San Antonio	1985–	Sarah Weddington Austin	1973–1979

House of Representatives

Edith E. Wilmans Dallas	1923–1925	Wilhelmina Delco Austin	1975–
Helen Moore Texas City	1929–1933 1935–1937	Susan G. McBee Del Rio	1975–1983
Mrs. Lee J. Rountree Bryan	1931–1933	Lou Nelle Sutton San Antonio	1976–
Sarah T. Hughes* Dallas	1931–1935	Betty Duncan Waco	1977–
Mrs. N. R. Strong Slocum	1931–1933	Ernestine Glossbrenner Alice	1977–
Neveille H. Colson Navasota	1939–1949	Irma Rangel Kingsville	1977–
Margaret H. Gordon Waco	1939–1941	Mary Jane Bode Austin	1977–1981
Ray Files Waxahachie	1941–1951	Lanelle Cofer Dallas	1977–1983
Florence Fenley Uvalde	1943–1947	Anita Hall Dallas	1979–
Elizabeth Suiter Winnsboro	1943–1949	Mary Polk El Paso	1979–1984
Mrs. A. R. (Robin) Henderson Groesbeck	1949–1951	Debra Danburg Houston	1981–
Virginia Duff Ferris	1951–1963	Patricia Hill Dallas	1983–
Dorothy G. Gurley Del Rio	1951–1955	Jan McKenna Arlington	1983–
Anita Blair El Paso	1953–1955	Phyllis Robinson Gonzales	1983–
Maud Isaacs El Paso	1954–1967	Gwyn Clarkson Shea Dallas	1983–
Myra D. Banfield Rosenberg	1961–1963	Nancy McDonald El Paso	1984–
Mrs. Sue Hairgrove Lake Jackson	1967–1969	Anne Cooper San Marcos	1985–
		Lena Guerrero Austin	1985–

* Elected to a third term, but resigned when appointed a state district judge.

CREDITS

NOTE: All locations are in Texas unless otherwise indicated.

Page 2. Wichita woman: Barker Texas History Center, UT-Austin.

Page 4. Woman preparing buffalo hide: National Anthropological Archives, Smithsonian Institution, negative #3700.

Page 5. Women constructing tepee: Richard Pohrt, Flint, Mich.

Page 5. Women with travois: U. T. Institute of Texan Cultures at San Antonio.

Page 6. Angelina: Painting by Ancel Nunn; reproduced courtesy of Claude Smitheart, Lufkin.

Page 7. Winnie Richards, member of the Tonkawa tribe: National Anthropological Archives, Smithsonian Institution, negative #1196-B.

Page 8. Cynthia Ann Parker and Prairie Flower, 1862. Texas Collection, Baylor University, Waco.

Page 8. Sallie Reynolds Matthews: Watt R. Matthews, Albany; copy from U. T. Institute of Texan Cultures.

Page 9. Comanche family, c. 1888. Western History Collections, University of Oklahoma Library, W. S. Campbell Collection, negative #196.

Page 10. María Jesús de Agreda: U. T. Institute of Texan Cultures.

Page 11. Augustina de León Alderete (great-granddaughter of Doña Patricia de la Garza de León and Don Martín de León) and her husband: Henry Hauschild, Victoria.

Page 12. Doña Calvillo, white stallion: Drawing by Thom Ricks; copy from U. T. Institute of Texan Cultures.

Page 12. Landowner and overseer: Copy from a 19th century illustration; U. T. Institute of Texan Cultures.

Page 13. Canary Island descendants: *The San Antonio Light* Collection, U. T. Institute of Texan Cultures.

Page 14. Women and boy selling birds: The Library of the Daughters of the Republic of Texas at the Alamo.

Page 15. Jane Long: Winston Farber, Houston; copy from U. T. Institute of Texan Cultures.

Page 15. Descendants of Kian Long: Grant Prater, Galveston; copy from U. T. Institute of Texan Cultures.

Page 16. Mary and John Rabb: Barker Texas History Center, UT-Austin.

Page 17. Mary Austin Holley: Barker Texas History Center, UT-Austin.

Page 18. Dilue Rose Harris: San Jacinto Museum of History Association, La Porte.

Page 19. Suzanna Dickinson: Barker Texas History Center, UT-Austin.

Page 19. Madame Andrea Candelaria: San Antonio Conservation Society.

Page 20. Girl with gun: Austin History Center, Austin (Texas) Public Library (C2800 PIC A 7307).

Page 20. "Yellow Rose of Texas" sheet music: Archives Division, Texas State Library.

Page 21. Angelina Eberly: U. T. Institute of Texan Cultures.

Page 22. Unidentified woman: Mrs. Annie R. Lee, San Antonio; copy from U. T. Institute of Texan Cultures.

Page 22. Mary Madison petition: Archives Division, Texas State Library.

Page 23. Cotton pickers: Schomburg Center for Research in Black Culture, New York Public Library, The Astor, Lenox and Tilden Foundations.

Page 24. Woman chopping cotton: Photograph by Dorothea Lange; courtesy of Schomberg Center for Research in Black Culture, New York Public Library.

Page 25. Adeline Waldon: WPA Records, Texas Slave Narratives (4H 361), Barker Texas History Center, UT-Austin.

Page 26. Matilda Boozie Randon and her husband the Reverend Eli Randon, holding their grandson George: Annie Mae Hunt, Dallas.

Page 28. Sophia Coffee Porter: *The Denison Herald*.

Page 29. Elise Waerenskjold: U. T. Institute of Texan Cultures.

Page 30. Sarah Archer: Barker Texas History Center, UT-Austin.

Page 30. Mariah Carr: Archives Division, Texas State Library.

Page 31. Lizzie Scott Neblett: Barker Texas History Center, UT-Austin.

Page 31. Unknown slave woman, Colorado County: South Central Texas Slavery Research Project, Winedale Historical Center.

Page 32. Black family celebrating Juneteenth: Austin History Center, Austin (Texas) Public Library (PIC A 05476).

Page 33. Title page of *The Freedman's Spelling-Book* (1866; reprint, New York: AMS Press, 1981).

Page 34. Lizzie Johnson Williams and Hezekiel Williams: Austin History Center, Austin (Texas) Public Library (PIC B 09912).

Page 35. Henrietta King: Photography Collection, Harry Ransom Humanities Research Center, UT-Austin.

Page 35. Emma Dehouch (Mrs. Pierre Van) Hollebeke and her three sons, Culberson County: Mrs. Rosa Belle Cooksey, Pecos; copy from U. T. Institute of Texan Cultures.

Page 36. Ellen O'Toole Corrigan: Mary Corrigan Walker, San Antonio; copy from U. T. Institute of Texan Cultures.

Page 36. Workers on the La Mota Ranch, LaSalle County, c. 1880s: Virginia Sturges and Amanda Newman, Cotulla; copy from U. T. Institute of Texan Cultures.

Page 36. Johanna Carolyn Pugel Wilhelm: John F. Wilhelm Estate; copy from U. T. Institute of Texan Cultures.

Page 37. Santos Chavarría: Archives of the Big Bend, Sul Ross State University, Alpine.

Page 37. Ear marks, Nueces County Brand Records, Book B, 1867, 1868, 1869. Copy from Hortense Warner Ward, "Indian Sign on the Spaniard's Cattle," in *From Hell to Breakfast*, ed. Mody Boatright (Dallas: SMU Press for the Texas Folklore Society, 1967).

Page 38. Elisabet Ney: Archives Division, Texas State Library.

Page 38. Bust of Sam Houston, sculpted by Elisabet Ney: Photograph by Sherry A. Smith, Austin.

Page 39. Louise Wueste at age 78: Stella Tylor Estate; copy from U. T. Institute of Texan Cultures.

Page 40. Mother Madeleine Chollet: Archives, Incarnate Word Generalate, San Antonio.

Page 41. Nurses in a ward at Santa Rosa Hospital, San Antonio: Santa Rosa Medical Center, San Antonio.

Page 42. Fannie Breedlove Davis: Woman's Missionary Union, Auxiliary to Baptist General Convention of Texas, Dallas.

Page 43. Dr. Maud A. B. Fuller: Ebenezer Baptist Church, Austin.

Page 44. Martha McWhirter and the Belton Sanctificationists: Dayton Kelley Collection, Salado; copy from U. T. Institute of Texan Cultures.

Page 45. Mrs. C. C. de la Garza: *The San Antonio Light* Collection, U. T. Institute of Texan Cultures.

Page 45. Helena Landa: Mrs. Robert Murray, San Antonio; copy from U. T. Institute of Texan Cultures.

Page 46. Melinda Rankin: Copy from Kate Miller Johnson, "Some Pioneer Women Teachers in Texas Before 1860," Thesis, UT-Austin, 1929; copy from General Libraries, UT-Austin.

Page 47. Mrs. Thomas J. (Mattie B.) White: Carver Museum, Austin; copy from U. T. Institute of Texan Cultures.

Page 47. Dolores Burton Linton: Courtesy of U.T. Institute of Texan Cultures.

Page 48. Olga Kohlberg: Texas Western Press, University of Texas at El Paso.

Page 48. Dallas Free Kindergarten, c. 1914: Texas/Dallas History and Archives Division, Dallas Public Library.

Page 49. Leonór Villegas de Magnón's class in Laredo: Leonor Grubbs, Houston; courtesy of Ellen C. Temple, publisher; copy from M. B. Rogers et al., *We Can Fly: Stories of Katherine Stinson and Other Gutsy Texas Women* (Austin: Ellen C. Temple, 1983).

Page 49. Leonór Villegas de Magnón: Leonor Grubbs, Houston; courtesy of Ellen C. Temple, publisher; copy from M. B. Rogers et al., *We Can Fly: Stories of Katherine Stinson and Other Gutsy Texas Women* (Austin: Ellen C. Temple, 1983).

Page 50. Belle Starr: Copy from *Bella Starr, The Bandit Queen*, facsimile edition (Austin: Steck Vaughn Company, 1960).

Page 52. Mary Maverick and her children: Copy from Rena Maverick Green, *Memoirs of Mary A. Maverick* (San Antonio: Alamo Printing, 1921).

Page 53. Freedwomen and children, McFadden Plantation, Circleville: Austin History Center, Austin (Texas) Public Library (N1600, PIC A 05496).

Page 54. *5000 Years in the Kitchen*: Cover of cookbook published by Sisterhood of Temple Emanu-El, Dallas, 1965: courtesy of Temple Emanu-El Sisterhood.

Page 54. Woman grinding on a metate: U. T. Institute of Texan Cultures.

Page 55. Annie Mae Hunt: Photograph by Eje Wray; copy from Ruthe Winegarten, ed., *I Am Annie Mae, The Personal Story of a Black Texas Woman* (Austin: Rosegarden Press, 1983).

Page 56. Woman and windmill: Archives of the Big Bend, Sul Ross State University, Alpine.

Page 56. Mary Ann Goodnight: Panhandle-Plains Historical Museum, Canyon.

Page 57. Lizzie Thurman: Courtesy of Cooke County Heritage Society.

Page 57. Woman and snake: Austin History Center, Austin (Texas) Public Library (Chalberg Collection #730).

Page 58. YWCA poster: YWCA, Dallas.

Page 58. Plainview office workers, c. 1923: Panhandle-Plains Historical Museum, Canyon.

Page 59. Dallas Main Central telephone switchboard, 1919: Southwestern Bell Telephone Company, St. Louis, Mo.

Page 60. Corpus Christi Beauty Shop: Photography Collection, Harry Ransom Humanities Research Center, UT-Austin.

Page 61. Ruth Morris, student in the household efficiency class, San Antonio YWCA: *The San Antonio Light* Collection, U. T. Institute of Texan Cultures.

Page 62. "Curandera II,": Etching 1979 by Carmen Lomas Garza, San Francisco.

Page 62. Elizabeth Boyle "Aunt Hank" Smith: Crosby County Pioneer Memorial Museum, Crosbyton.

Page 62. Black midwives, c. 1922: Southwest Center for Nursing History, UT-Austin School of Nursing.

Page 63. John Sealy Hospital School for Nurses, Galveston: Moody Medical Library, The University of Texas Medical Branch at Galveston.

Page 63. A. Louise Dietrich: Southwest Center for Nursing History, UT-Austin School of Nursing.

Page 64. Adina de Zavala: Barker Texas History Center, UT-Austin.

Page 64. Dallas High School students in a joinery shop, 1908: Texas/Dallas History and Archives Division, Dallas Public Library.

Page 65. Dorothy Robinson and her class: Courtesy of Madrona Press; copy from Dorothy Robinson, *The Bell Rings at Four; A Black Teacher's Chronicle of Change* (Austin: Madrona Press, 1978).

Page 65. Dr. Annie Webb Blanton: U. T. Institute of Texan Cultures; copy from *Pioneer Women Teachers of Texas* (Austin: Gammaway Print for Delta Kappa Gamma Society, 1952).

Page 65. Dr. Mary Elizabeth Branch: Huston-Tillotson College, Austin.

Page 66. Mary Elizabeth (Mrs. Lee) Bivins, Amarillo: Personal family pictures, Bivins Family, Amarillo.

Page 66. Ada Simond on her 80th birthday on the lawn of the Texas State Capitol: copyright Alan Pogue, Austin.

Page 67. Dallas Public Library interior: Texas/Dallas History and Archives Division, Dallas Public Library.

Page 67. Julia Ideson: Courtesy of Houston Metropolitan Research Center, Houston Public Library.

Page 68. Ada Anderson (second from left) judges food for a 4-H Club, 1946: Courtesy of Ada C. Anderson, Austin.

Page 68. Dr. Mary Gearing: Archives, Department of Home Economics, UT-Austin.

Page 70. Dr. Clotilde Page Garcia examines a child with the assistance of her nurse Isabel Montes, 1985: Courtesy of Dr. Clotilde Page Garcia, Corpus Christi.

Page 71. Dr. Sofie Herzog: Archives Division, Texas State Library.

Page 71. Dr. Connie Yerwood Conner: Courtesy of Dr. Connie Yerwood Conner, Austin.

Page 72. All-Woman Supreme Court, Austin, Jan. 5, 1925: Texas State Archives; copy from U. T. Institute of Texan Cultures.

Page 72. Frances Cox (Mrs. James Pinckney) Henderson: Barker Texas History Center, UT-Austin.

Page 73. Judge Sarah T. Hughes: U. T. Institute of Texan Cultures.

Page 73. Judge Gabrielle McDonald: Courtesy of Judge Gabrielle McDonald, Houston.

Page 73. Judge Elma Teresa Salinas: Courtesy of Judge Elma Salinas, Laredo.

Page 74. Dr. Mary S. Young and her donkey Nebuchadnezzar: Barker Texas History Center, UT-Austin; copy from *Southwestern Historical Quarterly* 65, no. 3 (1961–62).

Page 75. Ynes Mexia: General Library, UT-Austin; copy from *Madrono* 4 (1929): 274.

Page 75. Dr. Ellen C. Furey, 1939: *The San Antonio Light* Collection, U. T. Institute of Texan Cultures.

Page 76. Mrs. S. A. Masterson, 1939: *The San Antonio Light* Collection, U. T. Institute of Texan Cultures.

Page 77. Clara McLaughlin: Courtesy of Clara McLaughlin, Houston.

Page 77. Jovita Idar (second from right) in the print shop of *El Progresso*, 1914: Jovita Lopez, San Antonio; courtesy of Ellen C. Temple, publisher; copy from M. B. Rogers et al., *We Can Fly* (Austin: Ellen C. Temple, 1983).

Page 78. Amelia Barr at the age of 80: Barker Texas History Center, UT-Austin; copy from Amelia Barr, *All the Days of My Life* (New York: Appleton & Co., 1913).

Page 78. Selma Metzenthin-Raunik: Courtesy of Mrs. Nolan H. Schulze; copy from U. T. Institute of Texan Cultures.

Page 79. Lucy Parsons: Chicago Historical Society.

Page 80. Maud Cuney-Hare: Barker Texas History Center, UT-Austin; copy from Maud Cuney-Hare, *Norris Wright Cuney* (New York: Crisis Pub., 1913).

Page 81. Cover of *Sor Juana and Other Plays*, written by Estela Portillo Trambley of El Paso: Courtesy of Bilingual Press, SUNY Binghampton, New York, 1983.

Page 81. Dorothy Scarborough: Texas Collection, Baylor University, Waco.

Page 82. Corinne De Viney, Caldwell County, 1939: *The San Antonio Light* Collection, U. T. Institute of Texan Cultures.

Page 82. Girl selling lemonade: Encino Press; copy from A. C. Greene, *Dallas, the Deciding Years* (Austin: Encino Press, 1973).

Page 83. Mr. and Mrs. C. J. Washmon in front of their store, Mesquite: Copy from *A Stake in the Prairie: Mesquite, Texas* (Mesquite Historical Society, 1984).

Page 83. Florence Butt: Courtesy of H. E. B. Foods-Drugs Stores, Corpus Christi.

Page 84. Mrs. A. W. Rysinger: Delta Sigma Theta Sorority, Inc., Austin Alumnae Chapter.

Page 84. Josephine Theis Millinery Shop, Austin: Austin History Center, Austin (Texas) Public Library (PIC B 09115).

Page 85. Carrie Marcus Neiman: Neiman-Marcus, Dallas.

Page 85. Edna, Louise, and Elsie Frankfurt (left to right): Texas/Dallas History and Archives Division, Dallas Public Library.

Page 86. Bette Graham (holding shovel) breaking ground for a new corporate headquarters in Dallas: Gihon Foundation, Dallas.

Page 86. Lucille Bishop Smith: Gladys Smith Hogan, Brenham.

Page 133. Woman carrying a basket of peppers: c Alan Pogue, Austin.

Page 134. U. S. Ambassador Anne Armstrong: Courtesy of Anne Armstrong, Armstrong, TX; copy from U. T. Institute of Texan Cultures.

Page 134. U. S. Ambassador to the United Nations Zelma George: United Nations, New York City; copy from U. T. Institute of Texan Cultures.

Page 135. Liz Carpenter: Courtesy of Liz Carpenter, Austin.

Page 136. Dr. Nikki Van Hightower, Houston: Houston Area Women's Center.

Page 136. Gerry Beer and the child of a battered mother: Courtesy of Gerry Beer, Dallas.

Page 137. Demonstration favoring the Equal Rights Amendment, Austin, 1975: Austin History Center, Austin (Texas) Public Library (W5100, PIC A 09932).

Page 137. Jane Hickie: Courtesy of Jane Hickie, Austin.

Page 138. Sarah Weddington: Courtesy of Sarah Weddington, Austin.

Page 138. Barbara Jordan: U. T. Institute of Texan Cultures.

Page 139. Campaign brochure of Frances Farenthold: Courtesy of Frances Farenthold, Houston.

Page 139. Martha Cotera: Courtesy of Martha Cotera, Austin.

Page 140. State Rep. Wilhelmina Delco: Courtesy of Wilhelmina Delco, Austin.

Page 140. State Rep. Irma Rangel: Courtesy of Irma Rangel, Kingsville.

Page 140. State Rep. Lena Guerrero: Photograph by Lucia Uhl, Austin.

Page 140. State Senator Cyndi Taylor Krier: *Austin American Statesman*, January 17, 1985.

Page 141. Emma Long: Austin History Center, Austin (Texas) Public Library (PIC A 13911).

Page 141. Carole Keeton Rylander: Courtesy of Carole Rylander, Austin.

Page 141. Kathy Whitmire: Courtesy of Kathy Whitmire, Houston.

Page 142. Texas Secretary of State Myra McDaniel, January 1985. Photograph by Bill Malone, Austin.

Page 143. Texas State Treasurer Ann W. Richards, June 1984. Photograph by Texas Senate Media Services.

Page 144. Texas Women's Hall of Fame: Photograph by Bill Malone, Austin.

Page 145. Mary Catherine McCabe riding a Marfa History Club World Peace Float, c. 1930s: Archives of the Big Bend, Sul Ross State University, Marfa.

Page 146. Austin women making a United Nations quilt, c. 1945–1946. Ada C. Anderson, Austin.

Page 147. Cordye Hall demonstrating against the Vietnam War, 1960s: Courtesy of Cordye Hall, Dallas.

Page 148. Idelle Rabin and Njeri Mungai, Kenya, 1985. Courtesy of Idelle Rabin, Dallas.

Page 148. Dr. Dorothea Brown (left) shaking hands with Dr. Guillermina Valdez, April 20, 1985, Austin: Photograph by Alan Pogue, Austin.

Page 149. Suey Gee Eng and Yuck Lon Leung: *The San Antonio Light* Collection, U. T. Institute of Texan Cultures.

Page 150. Martha Lathan Pierce, Shelby County: Courtesy of Eakin Press; copy from Charles E. Tatum, *Shelby County* (Austin: Eakin Press, 1984), 133.

Page 150. Maria and Mersedes Cabazos (?), 1916. Courtesy of Mrs. Robert Rubio, San Antonio; copy from U. T. Institute of Texan Cultures.

Page 151. Martha Frances Winegarten, Dallas, 1956. Private collection of Ruthe Winegarten, Austin.

Page 152. Texas Woman's University basketball team, c. 1920s: Courtesy of the Texas Woman's University Library Archives, Denton.

Page 152. Stuart Female Academy students, Austin, c. 1900. Austin History Center, Austin (Texas) Public Library (AF P 7276 PIC A 05713).

Page 153. Two girls smoking: Austin History Center, Austin (Texas) Public Library (AF Biographical File PIC A 15549).

Page 153. L. C. Anderson High School: Austin History Center, Austin (Texas) Public Library (P 8620 PIC A 07567).

Page 154. Emily Burken: Courtesy of Women and Their Work, Austin.

Page 154. Dr. Hallie Earle, Waco: Texas Collection, Baylor University, Waco.

Page 154. Three ladies clowning: Austin History Center, Austin (Texas) Public Library (AF Biographical File PIC A 15520).

Page 155. Celia Cohen Lewin, Dallas: Private collection of Ruthe Winegarten, Austin.

Page 155. The wedding party of Hattie Campbell, Ebenezer Baptist Church, Austin, 1909. Austin History Center, Austin (Texas) Public Library.

Page 156. Mrs. Lucia Garcia de Guerrero: Courtesy of Mr. and Mrs. Julian C. Mungia, San Antonio; copy for U. T. Institute of Texan Cultures.

Page 156. Wichita women and baby: National Anthropological Archives, Smithsonian Institution, negative 1338-A.

Page 157. A Dallas family, Max and Jenny Cohen and daughters: Private collection of Ruthe Winegarten, Austin.

Page 158. Women's Progressive Club, San Antonio: Courtesy of Lillian W. Sutton-Taylor, San Antonio; copy from U. T. Institute of Texan Cultures.

Page 159. St. Vincent de Paul nurses, Dallas: Courtesy of St. Paul Medical Center, Dallas.

Page 160. Rosa von Roeder Kleberg and family: Barker Texas History Center, UT-Austin.

Page 161. Cecilia Rucker Collins, Travis County: Courtesy of Ada C. Anderson, Austin.

Page 161. Rosa Granillo: Courtesy of Cleofas Calleros Estate; copy from U. T. Institute of Texan Cultures.

Page 162. Ginger Rogers at exhibit opening, San Antonio, 1961: Courtesy of Texas Foundation for Women's Resources, Austin.

Page 162. Lydia Mendoza: Courtesy Lydia Mendoza, Houston.

NOTES

All factual information in this book was taken from the files of the Texas Women's History Project Exhibit Archives, located at the Texas Woman's University in Denton, Texas, except as indicated below. Those archives were compiled by collecting materials from libraries, museums, and individuals all across the state of Texas.

CHAPTER 1

Page 4. Alvar Nunez Cabeza de Vaca, *Relacion* (Zamora, Spain, 1542) quoted in John Upton Terrell and Donna M. Terrell, *Indian Women of the Western Morning* (Garden City, N. Y.: Anchor Press, 1976), 36; Carolyn Niethammer, *Daughters of the Earth* (New York: Collier Books, 1977), 112–114.

Page 5. Ferdinand Roemer, *Texas*, trans. Oswald Mueller (1849; reprint, San Antonio: n.p., 1935), 106.

Page 6. Fray Gaspar de Solis, "Diary of a Visit of Inspection of the Texas Missions in the Year 1767–1768," trans. Margaret Kenney Kress, *Southwestern Historical Quarterly* 35, no. 1 (1931): 61. Other quotations are from Diane H. Corbin, "Angelina," in *Legendary Ladies of Texas*, ed. F. E. Abernethy (Dallas: E-Heart Press, 1981), 15–19. Also see Patricia Lynn Spears, *Angelina* (Austin: Eakin, 1984); W. W. Newcomb, Jr., *Indians of Texas* (Austin: UT Press, 1961), 270–271.

Page 8. Jane Cazneau (McManus), *Eagle Pass; or Life on the Border by Cora Montgomery* (New York: Putnam, 1852), 187; Angie Debo, "Cynthia Ann Parker," in *Notable American Women*, ed. Edward T. James et al (Cambridge: Belknap Press of Harvard University Press, 1971), 3:15–16; "The Reminiscences of Mrs. Dilue Harris," *Quarterly of the Texas State Historical Association*, 4 (January 1901): 119; Crystal Sasse Ragsdale, "Mathilda Doebbler Gruen Wagner," *The Golden Free Land* (Austin: Landmark Press, 1976), 162; Sallie Reynolds Matthews, *Interwoven: A Pioneer Chronicle* (reprint, Austin: UT Press, 1974), 47.

Page 10. For an overview of Hispanic women's history, see Martha Cotera, *Diosa y Hembra: The History and Heritage of Chicanas in the U. S.* (Austin: Information Systems, 1976). Abernethy, "María de Agreda," in *Legendary Ladies of Texas*, 8–14; Janelle Scott, "Doña Patricia de la Garza de Leon," unpublished manuscript, Texas Women's History Project Archives, Biographical File, Texas Woman's University, Denton.

Page 12. Dr. D. Jeanne Callihan, "Doña María del Calvillo," in *Our Mexican Ancestors* (San Antonio: Institute of Texan Cultures, 1981), 1:49–54; Edith Parker, "Maria Gertrudis Cassiano," in *Women in Early Texas*, ed. Evelyn M. Carrington (Austin: Jenkins Publishing Co., 1975), 49–57; Minnie Gilbert, "Texas' First Cattle Queen [María Hinojosa de Balli]," in *Roots by the River* (Mission, Tex.: Border Kingdom Press, 1978), 15–25.

Page 13. María Betancour will, Bexar County Archives, San Antonio.

Page 14. Information about María Josefa Granados in Edward S. Sears, "The Low Down on Jim Bowie," in Mody Boatright, *From Hell to Breakfast* (Dallas: SMU Press for the Texas Folklore Society, 1934), 176.

Page 15. Ellen Garwood, "Early Texas Inns: A Study in Social Relationships," *Southwestern Historical Quarterly* 60, no. 2 (1956): 219–244; "J. C. Clopper's Journal and Book of Memoranda for 1828," *Southwestern Historical Quarterly* 13 (July 1909): 59–60.

Page 16. Mary Crownover Rabb, *Travels and Adventures in Texas in the 1820s, being the Reminiscences of M. C. Rabb* (Waco: W. M. Morrison, 1962), 14; Margaret Henson, *Anglo American Women in Texas, 1820–1850* (Boston: American Press, 1982); Ann Patton Malone, *Women on the Texas Frontier: A Cross-Cultural Perspective* (El Paso: Texas Western Press, 1983); Sandra L. Myres, *Westering Women and the Frontier Experience* (Albuquerque: University of New Mexico Press, 1982); Jo Ella Powell Exley, *Texas Tears and Texas Sunshine: Voices of Frontier Women* (College Station: Texas A&M Press, 1985).

Page 17. Mary Austin Holley, *Texas* (Lexington, Ky.: J. Clarke & Co., 1836), 40, 66, 78. Mary Austin Holley, *Texas, Observations Historical, Geographical, and Descriptive in a Series of Letters* (Baltimore: Armstrong and Plaskitt, 1833), 70, 84, 123–125.

Page 18. "Reminiscences of Mrs. Dilue Harris," quoted in Exley, *Texas Tears and Texas Sunshine*, 55, 58–59. Runaway Scrape anecdote: "Recollections of S. F. Sparks," *Southwestern Historical Quarterly* 12 (1908–1909), 63.

Page 19. Robert L. Ables, "The Second Battle for the Alamo," *Southwestern Historical Quarterly* 70, no. 3 (1967): 372–413.

Page 20. Martha Anne Turner, *The Yellow Rose of Texas: Her Saga and Song* (Austin: Shoal Creek, 1976).

Page 21. Tom Reilly, "Jane McManus Storms (Cazneau): Letters from the Mexican War, 1846–1848," *Southwestern Historical Quarterly*, 85 (July 1981): 21–44; Cazneau Papers, Barker Texas History Center, UT-Austin; Teresa Viele, *Following the Drum: A Glimpse of Frontier Life* (Lincoln: University of Nebraska Press, 1984), 21; L. W. Kemp, "Mrs. Angelina B. Eberly," *Southwestern Historical Quarterly* 36, no. 3 (1933): 193–199.

Pages 22–24. Alwyn Barr, *Black Texans: A History of Negroes in Texas, 1528–1971* (Austin: Jenkins, 1973); Dr. Rose Brewer, "Black Women in Texas: A Concept Paper," unpublished manuscript, Texas Women's History Project Archives, Topic File, TWU; Harold Schoen, "The Free Negro in the Republic of Texas," *Southwestern Historical Quarterly* 39, no. 4 (1936): 292–308; 40, no. 1 (1936): 26–34, 85–113; 40, no. 4 (1937): 267–289; "Mother was treated horrid" quotation in *Historical Outline of the Negro in Travis County*, ed. J. Mason Brewer (Austin: Samuel Huston College, 1940), 14; Bert J. Loewenberg and Ruth Bogin, "Louisa Picquet," in *Black Women in Nineteenth-Century American Life* (University Park: Pennsylvania State University Press, 1976), 54–69; John William Rogers, *The Lusty Texans of Dallas* (New York: Dutton, 1951), 92.

Page 25. Max S. Lale and Randolph B. Campbell, "The Plantation Journal of John B. Webster, Feb. 17, 1858–Nov. 5, 1859," *Southwestern Historical Quarterly* 84 (July 1980): 49–77. Quotation by Rosie Williams in Jakie L. Pruett and Everett B. Cole, *As We Lived: Stories by Black Story Tellers* (Burnet: Eakin, 1982), 73. Quotation by Mary Gaffney in *The American Slave, A Composite Autobiography*, ed. George Rawick (Westport, Conn.: Greenwood Press, 1972), 5, pt. 4: 1453. "An Overseer Named Minerva" in *Victorian*

Lady on the Texas Frontier: The Journal of Ann Raney Coleman, ed. C. Richard King (Norman: University of Oklahoma Press, 1971), 51.

Page 26. Ruthe Winegarten, ed., *I Am Annie Mae [Hunt]: The Personal Story of a Black Texas Woman* (Austin: Rosegarden Press, 1983), 5, 13–15.

CHAPTER 2

Page 27. See notes for page 29.

Page 28. Eudora Moore quotation in Exley, *Texas Tears and Texas Sunshine*, 147.

Page 29. Elise Waerenskjold, *Lady with the Pen*, ed C. A. Clausen (Clifton: Bosque Memorial Museum, 1976), vii, 20; Matthews, *Interwoven*, 30. Quotation from Claire Feller in Don H. Biggers, *German Pioneers in Texas* (1925; reprint, Austin: Eakin, 1983), 76–77. Melinda Rankin anecdote in William Stuart Red, *A History of the Presbyterian Church in Texas* (Austin: Steck, 1936), 329–331. Amelia Barr, *All the Days of My Life, An Autobiography* (New York: D. Appleton, 1913), 227.

Page 30. Harriet Person Perry quotation in Frances B. Simkins, *Women of the Confederacy* (Richmond and New York: Garrett & Massie, 1936), 150.

Page 31. Letter from Jenny to Lizzie Scott Neblett, March 23, 1862, Neblett Papers, Box 2F 81, Barker Texas History Center, UT-Austin; Fanny Norflet letter, December 28, 1862, Harriet Person Perry Papers, Duke University, Durham, N. C.

Page 32. Information about sharecropping arrangements in Lawrence D. Rice, *Negro in Texas, 1874–1900* (Baton Rouge: Louisiana State University Press, 1971), 167–168.

Page 33. Esther Lane Thompson, "The Influence of the Freedmen's Bureau on the Education of the Negro in Texas" (thesis, Texas Southern University, 1956); Robert C. Morris, *Reading, 'Riting, and Reconstruction: The Education of Freedmen in the South, 1861–1870* (Chicago: University of Chicago Press, 1981).

Pages 34–37. Emily Jones Shelton, "Lizzie E. Johnson: A Cattle Queen of Texas," *Southwestern Historical Quarterly* 50, no. 3 (1947): 349–366; "Steamboat Captain and Rancher: Captain John M. King," in *Roots by the River*, 51; Glen E. Lich, *The German Texans* (San Antonio: Institute of Texan Cultures, 1981), 110–111; "Mabel Doss Day Lea," in *Texas Women's Hall of Fame*, ed. Sinclair Moreland (Austin: Biographical Press, 1917).

Pages 39–40. Catherine McDowell, *Letters from the Ursuline, 1852–1853* (San Antonio: Trinity University Press for the Daughters of the Republic of Texas, 1977); Marjory Goar, *Marble Dust: The Life of Elisabet Ney* (Austin: Eakin, 1984).

Pages 42–43. Inez Boyle Hunt, *Century One, A Pilgrimage of Faith: Woman's Missionary Union 1880–1980* (Dallas: Woman's Missionary Union, Auxiliary to Baptist General Convention of Texas, 1980); Annie Doom Pickrell, *Pioneer Women in Texas* (Austin: Steck, 1929), 223; Maud A. B. Fuller, ed., *Guide for Woman's Home and Foreign Missionary Societies and Circles* (Austin: General Baptist Convention, n.d.).

Pages 44–45. Mrs. Fannie Heartsill Papers, Box 2D 273, Barker Texas History Center, UT-Austin; Willie Lee Lewis, *Between Sun and Sod: An Informal History of the Texas Panhandle* (1938; reprint, College Station: Texas A&M Press, 1976); George Nielsen, "Lydia McHenry and Revolutionary Texas," *Southwestern Historical Quarterly* 74, no. 3 (1971), 393–408; Frieda Werden, "Martha White McWhirter," in *Legendary Ladies of Texas*, ed. Abernethy,

115–122; Kay Turner, "Mexican-American Women's Home Altars," *lady-unique-inclination-of-the-night* (Autumn 1983): 71–81; "Jewish Texans" file, Institute of Texan Cultures, San Antonio.

Pages 46–47. Waerenskjold, *Lady with the Pen*; Melinda Rankin, *Texas in 1850* (1850; reprint, Austin: Texian Press, 1966), 116; Frederick Eby, *The Development of Education in Texas* (New York: MacMillan, 1925); Ruth Domatti, "A History of Kidd-Key College," *Southwestern Historical Quarterly* 63, no. 3 (1959): 262-78; Roberta Scott Ferguson, "The Education of Women and Girls in Texas Before the Civil War" (thesis, UT-Austin, 1925); Kate Miller Johnson, "Some Pioneer Women Teachers in Texas Before 1860" (thesis, UT-Austin, 1929); Bertie Barron letter, Texas Collection, Baylor University; John J. Lane, *History of Education in Texas*, U. S. Bureau of Education, Circular of Instruction, No. 2 (Washington, D. C.: Government Printing Office, 1903); Dolores Linton file, Institute of Texan Cultures, San Antonio; Mabelle Purcell, *Two Texas Female Seminaries* (Wichita Falls: Midwestern University Press, 1951); Dorothy Robinson, *The Bell Rings at Four: A Black Teacher's Chronicle of Change* (Austin: Madrona, 1978).

Pages 48–49. Mary S. Cunningham, *The Woman's Club of El Paso, Its First Thirty Years* (El Paso, UT-El Paso: Texas Western Press, 1978); *Dallas Free Kindergarten and Industrial Association Brochure*, 1916–1917 (at Dallas Historical Society); M. B. Rogers et al, "Women of a Revolution: Jovita Idar and Léonor Villegas de Magnón," in *We Can Fly* (Austin: Ellen C. Temple, 1983), 74–87; Emilio Zamoro, *Los Tejanos: Children of Two Cultures*, South Texas Head Start Bilingual-Bicultural Conference, South Texas Regional Training Office, Pan American University, Edinburg, January 5–6, 1978; *La Cronica* [Laredo], October 19, 1911.

Page 50. Ruthe Winegarten, "Belle Starr: The Bandit Queen of Dallas," in *Legendary Ladies of Texas*, ed. Abernethy, 38–49; Margaret H. Davis, "Harlots and Hymnals: A Historic Confrontation of Vice and Virtue in Waco, Texas," *Midsouth Folklore* 4 (Winter 1976); J. T. Upchurch, *Traps for Girls and Those Who Set Them: An Address to Men Only* (Arlington: Purity Pub., 1908).

CHAPTER 3

Pages 52–53. Mary A. Maverick, *Memoirs of Mary A. Maverick*, ed. Rena Maverick Green (San Antonio: Alamo Printing, 1921), 56–57, 98–99; Elizabeth Carpenter Diary, Plano Public Library; Mrs. Rowland Clyde Burns Diary, Southwest Collection, Texas Tech University.

Page 55. Winegarten, *I Am Annie Mae*, 67, 83–85, 115.

Pages 56–57. "The Women of the JA Ranch: Cornelia Adair and Molly Goodnight," in Rogers, *We Can Fly*, 126–139; "Lulu V. Jones," in Pruett and Cole, *As We Lived*, 93, 96. Quotation about digging for wood: Laura Hamner, *Short Grass and Longhorns* (Norman: University of Oklahoma Press, 1943), 9. "My job was to climb the tower" quotation in Patricia Cooper and Norma Buferd, *The Quilters* (Garden City, N. Y.: Doubleday, 1977), 36. "Reminiscences of C. C. Cox," *Texas Historical Association Quarterly* 6 (1902–1903): 116–117. Tilda Mae Holman quotation in Charles Tatum, *Shelby County* (Austin: Eakin, 1984), 40.

Pages 62–63. Pickrell, *Pioneer Women in Texas*, 103–107; Eleanor Crowder, *Nursing in Texas: A Pictorial History* (Waco: Texian Press, 1980).

Page 64. Patricia Ward Wallace, "Willie House," in *A Spirit So Rare* (Austin: Nortex, 1984), 181–187; Virginia Taylor, "Adina de Zavala," in *Women in Early Texas*, ed. Carrington.

Page 65. "Annie Webb Blanton," in *This Is Texas*, ed.

Mabelle Purcell and Stuart Purcell et al (Austin: Lel Purcell Hawkins, 1977); Olive Brown and Michael R. Heintze, "Mary Branch: Private College Educator," in *Black Leaders: Texans for Their Times*, ed. Alwyn Barr and Robert A. Calvert (Austin: Texas State Historical Association, 1981).

Page 68. Kate Adele Hill, *Home Demonstration Work in Texas, 1915–1955* (San Antonio: Naylor, 1958).

CHAPTER 4

Page 69. Mary Escher and Mary Sweeney information, Brazoria County Historical Survey Committee, Family Records, File 25.

Pages 70–71. "The Daring Doctor of Brazoria, Dr. Sofie Herzog," in Rogers, *We Can Fly*, 38–47; Sylvia Ferris and Eleanor Hoppe, *Scalpels and Sabers: Nineteenth Century Medicine in Texas* (Austin: Eakin, 1985), 197–205; Dr. Kenneth Aynesworth, to Lillian Bedichek, 1933 letter, Moody Medical Library Archives, UT-Medical Branch at Galveston; Dr. Leslie Waggener quotation in Larry J. Wygant, "A Note on the Early Medical Education of Women at UTMB," *The Bookman* [Moody Medical Library], March 1980; Mrs. George Plunkett Red, "Petticoat Medicine," in *The Medicine Man in Texas* (Houston: Standard Printing, 1930), 104–110.

Pages 72–73. Sue M. Hall, "The 1925 All-Women Supreme Court of Texas," unpublished paper, St. Mary's University School of Law, San Antonio, 1978; Hattie L. Henenberg, "Women of the Supreme Court of Texas," *Women Lawyers' Journal*, 19 (August 1932): 16; Mary D. Farrell and Elizabeth Silverthorne, "Frances Cox Henderson," in *First Ladies of Texas* (Belton: Stillhouse Hollow Pubs., 1976), 64–75; Ann Fears Crawford and Crystal Sasse Ragsdale, *Women in Texas* (Austin: Eakin, 1982); Patricia Lasher and Beverly Bentley, *Texas Women: Interviews & Images* (Austin: Shoal Creek, 1980).

Pages 74–75. Dr. Mary Sophie Young's journal in *Southwestern Historical Quarterly* 65, no. 3 (1961–1962): 386; Dr. Mary S. Young, *A Key to the Families and Genera of Flowering Plants and Ferns in the Vicinity of Austin, Texas*, University of Texas Bulletin, No. 1754, Sept. 25, 1917; Dr. Mary S. Young, *The Seed Plants, Ferns, and Fern Allies of the Austin Region*, University of Texas Bulletin, No. 2065, Nov. 20, 1920; Maud Jeannie Young, *Familiar Lessons in Botany* (New York: Barnes, 1873); "Ynes Mexia de Reyades," in Doris Hollis Pemberton, *Juneteenth at Comanche Crossing* (Austin: Eakin, 1983), 132–138; Elizabeth Sthreshley biography, Austin History Center, Austin Public Library.

Pages 76–81. Mrs. E. Spann, ed., *The Texian Monthly Magazine* 1, no. 1 (July 1858); Imogene Bentley Dickey, *Early Literary Magazines of Texas* (Austin: Steck-Vaughn, 1970); "Dorothy Renick," in Wallace, *A Spirit So Rare*, 204–209; Clara McLaughlin, *Black Parent's Handbook* (New York: Harcourt, Brace, 1976); Barr, *All the Days of My Life*, foreword; Amelia Barr, *Remember the Alamo* (New York: Dodd, Mead, 1888); Carolyn Ashbaugh, *Lucy Parsons: American Revolutionary* (Chicago: Charles Kerr for the Illinois Labor History Society, 1976); Maud Cuney-Hare, *Norris Wright Cuney: A Tribune of the Black People* (New York: Crisis Pub., 1913); Estela Portillo Trambley, *Sor Juana and Other Plays* (Ypsilanti, Mich.: Bilingual Press, 1983); Estela Portillo Trambley, "The Day of the Swallows," *El Grito* 4 (Spring 1971): 4–47; E. E. Mireles, R. B. Fisher, and Jovita G. Mireles, *Mi Libro Espanol* (Austin: Benson & Co., 1941); Jovita Gonzales de Mireles, "After the Barbed Wire Came Hunger," in *Aztlan: An Anthology of Mexican American Literature*, ed. Stan Steiner (New York: Knopf, 1972); Dorothy Scarborough Collection, Texas Collection, Baylor University, Waco.

Page 84. Ada Simond, *Let's Pretend: Mae Dee and Her Family Go to Town* (Austin: Stevenson Press, 1977), 11, 39.

Page 86. "Bette Graham," in Rogers, *We Can Fly*, 88–97.

Page 87. Elizabeth Enstam, "The Reluctant Matriarch [Sarah Cockrell]," *D Magazine*, March 3, 1978; Sarah Cockrell Papers, Dallas Historical Society.

Page 88. "Margo Jones, the Director," in Rogers, *We Can Fly*, 48–61.

Page 90. "Estella Maxey," in Wallace, *A Spirit So Rare*, 214–218.

Page 91. Mary Bunton, *A Bride on the Old Chisholm Trail in 1886* (San Antonio: Naylor, 1939) quoted in Exley, *Texas Tears and Texas Sunshine*, 231; "W. Steinert's View of Texas in 1849 [entry for July 2, 1849]," *Southwestern Historical Quarterly* 80 (1976–1977).

Pages 93–96. "Babe Didrikson Zaharias," "Katherine Stinson," "Space Women, America's First Female Astronauts," in Rogers, *We Can Fly*, 10–37, 152–173.

CHAPTER 5

Pages 97–98. Fanny L. Armstrong, *To the Noon Rest: The Life, Work and Addresses of Mrs. Helen M. Stoddard* (Butler, Ind.: n.p., 1909); Mrs. William M. Baines, *The Texas White Ribboner* (n.p., 1915).

Page 99. Joyce Thompson, *Marking a Trail: A History of the Texas Woman's University* (Denton: TWU Press, 1982).

Page 100. Stella L. Christian, *History of the Texas Federation of Women's Clubs* (Houston: Texas Federation of Women's Clubs, 1919); Fannie C. Potter, *History of the Texas Federation of Women's Clubs, 1918–1938* (Denton: Texas Federation of Women's Clubs, 1941); Rebecca Richmond, *A Woman of Texas: Mrs. Percy V. Pennybacker* (San Antonio: Naylor, 1941), 169; Pennybacker Papers, Barker Texas History Center, UT-Austin.

Page 101. Jeffie Conner Papers, Texas Collection, Baylor University; Private collection, Mrs. Willie Lee Gay, Houston; Armye Jones, *The Madison County Recreation and Health Center for Negroes* (Madisonville, 1946); National Council of Negro Women Archives, Washington, D. C.

Page 102. Johnowene Brackenridge Menger, "M. Eleanor Brackenridge, 1837–1924" (thesis, Trinity University, San Antonio, 1964).

Page 103. Martha Anne Turner, *Clara Driscoll, An American Tradition* (Austin: Madrona, 1979); "Anna Hertzberg," in *Jewish Texans* (San Antonio: Institute of Texan Cultures, 1974), as well as the institute's files.

Page 104. Ella Caruthers Porter et al, *Texas Motherhood Magazine* (Dallas, 1910); Archives of Texas PTA, Austin.

Page 105. Jeffie O. A. Conner Papers, Texas Collection, Baylor University; Jose E. Limon, "El Primer Congreso Mexicanista de 1911: A Precursor to Contemporary Chicanismo," *Aztlan* (Spring and Fall 1974); "Jovita Idar and Léonor Villegas de Magnón," in Rogers, *We Can Fly*.

Page 106. Anna Dupree Papers, Houston Metropolitan Research Center, Houston Public Library; Eleanor Freed, "Dominique de Menil," *Texas Humanist* (Sept.–Oct. 1984).

Page 107. Edna Gladney information at the Edna Gladney Home Archives, Ft. Worth, Texas; Kate Ripley information at Life Planning/Health Services, Dallas;

"Silver Tea": Rabbi William Greenberg, "History of the Jews in Dallas," *The Reform Advocate*, January 2, 1914, 3–21.

Page 109. Louise Iscoe, *Ima Hogg: First Lady of Texas* (Austin: Hogg Foundation for Mental Health, 1976); Virginia Bernhard, *Ima Hogg: The Governor's Daughter* (Austin: Texas Monthly Press, 1984).

CHAPTER 6

Pages 111–117. *Galveston Tribune*, June 14, 1913 [special suffrage edition]; A. Elizabeth Taylor, "The Woman Suffrage Movement in Texas," *Journal of Southern History* 17 (May 1951); John Eudy, "The Vote and Lone Star Women: Minnie Fisher Cunningham and the Texas Equal Suffrage Association," *East Texas Historical Journal* 14 (Fall 1976): 52–57; "Jane Y. McCallum" and "Christia Adair," in Rogers, *We Can Fly*, 98–125; Jacqueline Dowd Hall, *Revolt Against Chivalry: Jessie Daniel Ames and the Women's Campaign Against Lynching* (New York: Columbia University Press, 1979); Jane Y. McCallum Collection, Austin History Center, Austin Public Library; Minnie Fisher Cunningham Collection, Houston Metropolitan Research Center, Houston Public Library.

Page 118. Alfredo Mirande and Evangelina Enriquez, *La Chicana: The Mexican American Woman* (Chicago: University of Chicago Press, 1979), 206–207, 252.

Page 120. *Equal Rights* (National Women's Party), Washington, D. C., September 26, 1925.

Page 121. "The Flying Schoolmarm Marjorie Stinson," in Rogers, *We Can Fly*, 23.

Pages 122–123. Elizabeth W. Fernea, Marilyn P. Duncan et al, *Texas Women in Politics* (Austin: Foundation for Women's Resources, 1977).

Page 124. "Emma Tenayuca," *San Antonio Women's Magazine*, April 1985, 8–11.

Pages 126–127. Melissa Hield, "Women in the Texas ILGWU, 1933–1950," in *Speaking for Ourselves: Women of the South*, ed. Maxine Alexander (New York: Pantheon Books, 1984), 87–97.

Page 128. Juanita Craft Papers at Texas/Dallas History and Archives Division, Dallas Public Library; Cotera, *Diosa y Hembra*, 74–81; Maria Hernandez, *Mexico y los Cuatro Poderes Que Dirijen al Pueblo* (San Antonio: Munguia Printers, 1945).

Page 129. Fernea and Duncan, *Texas Women in Politics*.

CHAPTER 7

Pages 130–31. "Women's Airforce Service Pilots," in Rogers, *We Can Fly*, 140–151; "Lila Cockrell" and "Oveta Culp Hobby," in Lasher and Bentley, *Texas Women*, 36–41, 72–79; *Panther*, Prairie View A&M University Yearbook, 1943.

Page 134. "Anne Armstrong," in Lasher and Bentley, *Texas Women*, 1–5. Information on Zelma George in Marian Martinello and Melvin Sance, *A Personal History: The Afro-American Texans* (San Antonio: Institute of Texan Cultures, 1982), 76.

Page 136. Nancy Woloch, *Women and the American Experience* (New York: Knopf, 1984), 512–538.

Page 137. Texas Women's Meeting, *Summary of the Final Report to the National Commission on the Observance of International Women's Year by the Texas Coordinating Committee*, September 1977.

Pages 138–141. "Lila Cockrell," "Frances Farenthold," "Barbara Jordan," "Carole Keeton McClellan," and "Sarah Weddington," in Lasher and Bentley, *Texas Women*; Fernea and Duncan, *Texas Women in Politics*; "That Woman, Frances 'Sissy' Farenthold," "Congresswoman from Texas, Barbara Jordan," "Advisor to the President, Sarah Ragle Weddington," and "First Chicana Legislator, Irma Rangel," in Crawford and Ragsdale, *Women in Texas*.

Page 142. Mike Hailey, "New State Official [Myra McDaniel] Sets Vote Goal," *Austin American Statesman*, Sept. 17, 1984.

Page 143. Ruthe Winegarten, *Ann Richards, Texas State Treasurer: A Study of Her First Year in Office, 1983* (Austin: Texas Foundation for Women's Resources, 1983).

Page 144. Governor's Commission for Women, Austin, Texas files.

Page 145. Mrs. Lee Joseph quotation in Potter, *History of the Texas Federation of Women's Clubs*; Richmond, *A Woman of Texas*.

Page 146. Ruthe Winegarten, ed., "Cordye Hall, Texas Peacemother," unpublished oral history, private collection of Cordye Hall, Dallas, and Ruthe Winegarten, Austin.

BIBLIOGRAPHY

Books and Journals

Abernethy, F. E., ed. *Legendary Ladies of Texas*. Dallas: E-Heart, 1981.

Ables, Robert L. "The Second Battle for the Alamo." *Southwestern Historical Quarterly* 70, no. 3 (1967): 372–413.

Armstrong, Fanny L. *To the Noon Rest: The Life, Work and Addresses of Mrs. Helen M. Stoddard*. Butler, Ind.: n.p., 1909.

Ashbaugh, Carolyn. *Lucy Parsons: American Revolutionary*. Chicago: Charles Kerr for the Illinois Labor History Society, 1976.

Baines, Mrs. William M. *The Texas White Ribboner*. n.p., 1915.

Barr, Alwyn. *Black Texans: A History of Negroes in Texas, 1528–1971*. Austin: Jenkins, 1973.

Barr, Alwyn, and Robert A. Calvert, eds. *Black Leaders: Texans for Their Times*. Austin: Texas State Historical Association, 1981.

Barr, Amelia. *All the Days of My Life, An Autobiography*. New York: D. Appleton, 1913.

———. *Remember the Alamo*. New York: Dodd, Mead, 1888.

Bernhard, Virginia. *Ima Hogg: The Governor's Daughter*. Austin: Texas Monthly Press, 1984.

Biggers, Don H. *German Pioneers in Texas*. 1925. Reprint. Austin: Eakin, 1983.

Brewer, J. Mason, ed. *Historical Outline of the Negro in Travis County*. Austin: Samuel Huston College, 1940.

Brewer, Rose. "Black Women in Texas: A Concept Paper." Unpublished manuscript. Texas Women's History Project Archives, Topic File, TWU.

Bunton, Mary. *A Bride on the Old Chisholm Trail in 1886*. San Antonio: Naylor, 1939.

Cabeza de Vaca, Alvar Nunez. *Relacion*. Zamora, Spain, 1542. Quoted in John Upton Terrell and Donna M. Terrell. *Indian Women of the Western Morning*. Garden City, N. Y.: Anchor Press, 1976.

Callihan, D. Jeanne. "Doña María del Calvillo." In *Our Mexican Ancestors*. San Antonio: Institute of Texan Cultures, 1981.

Carrington, Evelyn M., ed. *Women in Early Texas*. Austin: Jenkins, 1975.

Cazneau, Jane. *Eagle Pass; or Life on the Border by Cora Montgomery*. New York: Putnam, 1852.

Christian, Stella L. *History of the Texas Federation of Women's Clubs*. Houston: Texas Federation of Women's Clubs, 1919.

Clopper, J. C. "J. C. Clopper's Journal and Book of Memoranda for 1828." *Southwestern Historical Quarterly* 13 (July 1909): 59–60.

Cooper, Patricia, and Norma Buferd. *The Quilters*. Garden City, N. Y.: Doubleday, 1977.

Cotera, Martha. *Diosa y Hembra: The History and Heritage of Chicanas in the U. S.* Austin: Information Systems, 1976.

Cox, C. C. "Reminiscences of C. C. Cox." *Texas Historical Association Quarterly* 6 (1902–1903): 116–17.

Crawford, Ann Fears, and Crystal Sasse Ragsdale. *Women in Texas*. Austin: Eakin, 1982.

Crowder, Eleanor. *Nursing in Texas: A Pictorial History*. Waco: Texian Press, 1980.

Cuney-Hare, Maud. *Norris Wright Cuney: A Tribune of the Black People*. New York: Crisis Pub., 1913.

Cunningham, Mary S. *The Women's Club of El Paso, Its First Thirty Years*. El Paso: UT-El Paso Texas Western Press, 1978.

Davis, Margaret H. "Harlots and Hymnals: A Historic Confrontation of Vice and Virtue in Waco, Texas," *Midsouth Folklore* 4 (Winter 1976).

Debo, Angie. "Cynthia Ann Parker." In *Notable American Women*, edited by Edward T. James et al. Cambridge: Belknap Press of Harvard University Press, 1971.

Dickey, Imogene Bentley. *Early Literary Magazines of Texas*. Austin: Steck-Vaughn, 1970.

Domatti, Ruth. "A History of Kidd-Key College." *Southwestern Historical Quarterly* 63, no. 3 (1959): 262–78.

Eby, Frederick. *The Development of Education in Texas*. New York: MacMillan, 1925.

"Emma Tenayuca." *San Antonio Women's Magazine*, April 1985, 8–11.

Enstam, Elizabeth. "The Reluctant Matriarch [Sarah Cockrell]." *D Magazine*, March 3, 1978.

Equal Rights (National Women's Party). Washington, D. C., September 26, 1925.

Eudy, John. "The Vote and Lone Star Women: Minnie Fisher Cunningham and the Texas Equal Suffrage Association." *East Texas Historical Journal* 14 (Fall 1976): 52–57.

Exley, Jo Ella Powell. *Texas Tears and Texas Sunshine: Voices of Frontier Women*. College Station: Texas A&M Press, 1985.

Farrell, Mary D., and Elizabeth Silverthorne. "Frances Cox Henderson." In *First Ladies of Texas*. Belton: Stillhouse Hollow Pubs., 1976.

Ferguson, Roberta Scott. "The Education of Women and Girls in Texas Before the Civil War." Thesis. UT-Austin, 1925.

Fernea, Elizabeth W., Marilyn P. Duncan et al. *Texas Women in Politics*. Austin: Foundation for Women's Resources, 1977.

Ferris, Sylvia, and Eleanor Hoppe. *Scalpels and Sabers: Nineteenth Century Medicine in Texas*. Austin: Eakin, 1985.

Freed, Eleanor. "Dominique de Menil." *Texas Humanist* (Sept.–Oct. 1984).

Fuller, Maud A. B., ed. *Guide for Women's Home and Foreign Missionary Societies and Circles*. Austin: General Baptist Convention, n.d.

Galveston Tribune, June 14, 1913 [special suffrage edition].

Garwood, Ellen. "Early Texas Inns: A Study in Social Relationships." *Southwestern Historical Quarterly* 60, no. 2 (1956): 219–44.

Gilbert, Minnie. "Texas' First Cattle Queen [María Hinojosa de Balli]." In *Roots by the River*. Mission, Tex.: Border Kingdom Press, 1978.

Goar, Marjory. *Marble Dust: The Life of Elisabet Ney*. Austin: Eakin, 1984.

Greenberg, Rabbi William. "History of the Jews in Dallas." *The Reform Advocate*, January 2, 1914, 3–21.

Hailey, Mike. "New State Official [Myra McDaniel] Sets Vote Goal." *Austin American Statesman*, Sept. 17, 1984.

Hall, Jacquelyn Dowd. *Revolt Against Chivalry: Jessie*

Daniel Ames and the Women's Campaign Against Lynching. New York: Columbia University Press, 1979.

Hall, Sue M. "The 1925 All-Women Supreme Court of Texas." Unpublished paper. St. Mary's University School of Law, San Antonio, 1978.

Hamner, Laura. *Short Grass and Longhorns.* Norman: University of Oklahoma Press, 1943.

Handbook of Texas in Two Volumes. Edited by Walter Prescott Webb. Austin: Texas State Historical Association, 1952.

Handbook of Texas. Volume 3. Edited by Eldon Branda. Austin: Texas State Historical Association, 1976.

Harris, Dilue. "The Reminiscences of Mrs. Dilue Harris." *Quarterly of the Texas State Historical Association* 4 (January 1901).

Henenberg, Hattie L. "Women of the Supreme Court of Texas." *Women Lawyers' Journal* 19 (August 1932).

Henson, Margaret. *Anglo American Women in Texas, 1820–1850.* Boston: American Press, 1982.

Hernandez, Maria. *Mexico y los Cuatro Poderes Que Dirijen al Pueblo.* San Antonio: Munguia Printers, 1945.

Hield, Melissa. "Women in the Texas ILGWU, 1933–1950." In *Speaking for Ourselves: Women of the South.* Edited by Maxine Alexander. New York: Pantheon Books, 1984.

Hill, Kate Adele. *Home Demonstration Work in Texas, 1915–1955.* San Antonio: Naylor, 1958.

Holley, Mary Austin. *Texas, Observations Historical, Geographical, and Descriptive in a Series of Letters.* Baltimore: Armstrong and Plaskitt, 1833.

Hunt, Inez Boyle. *Century One, A Pilgrimage of Faith: Woman's Missionary Union 1880–1980.* Dallas: Woman's Missionary Union, Auxiliary to Baptist General Convention of Texas, 1980.

Iscoe, Louise. *Ima Hogg: First Lady of Texas.* Austin: Hogg Foundation for Mental Health, 1976.

Jewish Texans. San Antonio: Institute of Texan Cultures, 1974.

Johnson, Kate Miller. "Some Pioneer Women Teachers in Texas Before 1860." Thesis. UT-Austin, 1929.

Jones, Armye. *The Madison County Recreation and Health Center for Negroes.* Madisonville, 1946.

Kemp, L. W. "Mrs. Angelina B. Eberly." *Southwestern Historical Quarterly* 36, no. 3 (1933): 193–99.

King, C. Richard, ed. *Victorian Lady on the Texas Frontier: The Journal of Ann Raney Coleman.* Norman: University of Oklahoma Press, 1971.

La Cronica [Laredo], October 19, 1911.

Lale, Max S., and Randolph B. Campbell. "The Plantation Journal of John B. Webster, Feb. 17, 1858–Nov. 5, 1859." *Southwestern Historical Quarterly* 84 (July 1980): 49–77.

Lane, John J. *History of Education in Texas.* U. S. Bureau of Education, Circular of Instruction, No. 2. Washington, D. C.: Government Printing Office, 1903.

Lasher, Patricia, and Beverly Bentley. *Texas Women: Interviews & Images.* Austin: Shoal Creek, 1980.

Lewis, Willie Lee. *Between Sun and Sod: An Informal History of the Texas Panhandle.* 1938. Reprint. College Station: Texas A&M Press, 1976.

Lich, Glen E. *The German Texans.* San Antonio: Institute of Texan Cultures, 1981.

Limon, Jose E. "El Primer Congreso Mexicanista de 1911: A Precursor to Contemporary Chicanismo." *Aztlan* (Spring and Fall 1974).

Loewenberg, Bert J., and Ruth Bogin. "Louisa Picquet." In *Black Women in Nineteenth-Century American Life.* University Park: Pennsylvania State University Press, 1976.

Malone, Ann Patton. *Women on the Texas Frontier: A Cross-Cultural Perspective.* El Paso: Texas Western Press, 1983.

Martinello, Marian, and Melvin Sance. *A Personal History: The Afro-American Texans.* San Antonio: Institute of Texan Cultures, 1982.

Matthews, Sallie Reynolds. *Interwoven: A Pioneer Chronicle.* Reprint. Austin: UT Press, 1974.

Maverick, Mary A. *Memoirs of Mary A. Maverick.* Edited by Rena Maverick Green. San Antonio: Alamo Printing, 1921.

McDowell, Catherine. *Letters from the Ursuline, 1852–1853.* San Antonio: Trinity University for the Daughters of the Republic of Texas, 1977.

McLaughlin, Clara. *Black Parent's Handbook.* New York: Harcourt, Brace, 1976.

Menger, Johnowene Brackenridge. "M. Eleanor Brackenridge, 1837–1924." Thesis. Trinity University, San Antonio, 1964.

Mirande, Alfredo, and Evangelina Enriquez. *La Chicana: The Mexican American Woman.* Chicago: University of Chicago Press, 1979.

Mireles, E. E., R. B. Fisher, and Jovita G. Mireles. *Mi Libro Espanol.* Austin: Benson & Co., 1941.

Mireles, Jovita Gonzales de. "After the Barbed Wire Came Hunger." In *Aztlan: An Anthology of Mexican American Literature.* Edited by Stan Steiner. New York: Knopf, 1972.

Moreland, Sinclair, ed. *Texas Women's Hall of Fame.* Austin: Biographical Press, 1917.

Morris, Robert C. *Reading, 'Riting, and Reconstruction: The Education of Freedmen in the South, 1861–1870.* Chicago: University of Chicago Press, 1981.

Myres, Sandra L. *Westering Women and the Frontier Experience.* Albuquerque: University of New Mexico Press, 1982.

Newcomb, W. W., Jr. *Indians of Texas.* Austin: UT Press, 1961.

Nielsen, George. "Lydia McHenry and Revolutionary Texas." *Southwestern Historical Quarterly* 74, no. 3 (1971), 393–408.

Niethammer, Carolyn. *Daughters of the Earth.* New York: Collier Books, 1977.

Panther. Prairie View A&M University Yearbook, 1943.

Pemberton, Doris Hollis. *Juneteenth at Comanche Crossing.* Austin: Eakin, 1983.

Pickrell, Annie Doom. *Pioneer Women in Texas.* Austin: Steck, 1929.

Porter, Ella Caruthers, et al. *Texas Motherhood Magazine.* Dallas, 1910.

Potter, Fannie C. *History of the Texas Federation of Women's Clubs, 1918–1938.* Denton: XXXX, 1941.

Pruett, Jakie L., and Everett B. Cole. *As We Lived: Stories by Black Story Tellers.* Burnet: Eakin, 1982.

Purcell, Mabelle. *Two Texas Female Seminaries.* Wichita Falls: Midwestern University Press, 1951.

Purcell, Mabelle, Stuart Purcell et al, eds. *This Is Texas.* Austin: Lel Purcell Hawkins, 1977.

Rabb, Mary Crownover. *Travels and Adventures in Texas in the 1820s, being the Reminiscences of M. C. Rabb.* Waco: W. M. Morrison, 1962.

Ragsdale, Crystal Sasse. *The Golden Free Land.* Austin: Landmark Press, 1976.

Rankin, Melinda. *Texas in 1850.* 1850. Reprint. Austin: Texian Press, 1966.

Rawick, George, ed. *The American Slave, A Composite Auto-biography.* Vol. 5, part 4. Westport, Conn.: Greenwood Press, 1972.

Red, Mrs. George Plunkett. "Petticoat Medicine." In *The Medicine Man in Texas.* Houston: Standard Printing, 1930.

Red, William Stuart. *A History of the Presbyterian Church in Texas.* Austin: Steck, 1936.

Reilly, Tom. "Jane McManus Storms (Cazneau): Letters from the Mexican War, 1846–1848." *Southwestern Historical Quarterly* 85 (July 1981): 21–44.

Rice, Lawrence D. *Negro in Texas, 1874–1900.* Baton Rouge: Louisiana State University Press, 1971.

Richmond, Rebecca. *A Woman of Texas: Mrs. Percy V. Pennybacker.* San Antonio: Naylor, 1941.

Robinson, Dorothy. *The Bell Rings at Four: A Black Teacher's Chronicle of Change.* Austin: Madrona, 1978.

Roemer, Ferdinand. *Texas.* Translated by Oswald Mueller. 1849. Reprint. San Antonio: n.p., 1935.

Rogers, John William. *The Lusty Texans of Dallas.* New York: Dutton, 1951.

Rogers, Mary Beth. *Texas Women: A Celebration of History Exhibit Catalog.* Austin: Texas Foundation for Women's Resources, 1981.

Rogers, Mary Beth, Sherry Smith, and Janelle Scott. *We Can Fly: Stories of Katherine Stinson and Other Gutsy Texas Women.* Austin: Ellen C. Temple, 1983.

Schoen, Harold. "The Free Negro in the Republic of Texas." *Southwestern Historical Quarterly* 39, no. 4 (1936): 292–308; 40, no. 1 (1936): 26–34, 85–113; 40, no. 4 (1937); 267–89.

Scott, Janelle. "Doña Patricia de la Garza de Leon." Unpublished manuscript. Texas Women's History Project Archives. Biographical File. Texas Woman's University, Denton.

Sears, Edward S. "The Low Down on Jim Bowie." In Mody Boatright. *From Hell to Breakfast.* Dallas: SMU Press for the Texas Folklore Society, 1934.

Shelton, Emily Jones. "Lizzie E. Johnson: A Cattle Queen of Texas." *Southwestern Historical Quarterly* 50, no. 3 (1947): 349–366.

Simkins, Frances B. *Women of the Confederacy.* Richmond and New York: Garrett & Massie, 1936.

Simond, Ada. *Let's Pretend: Mae Dee and Her Family Go to Town.* Austin: Stevenson Press, 1977.

Solis, Fray Gaspar de. "Diary of a Visit of Inspection of the Texas Missions in the Year 1767–68." Translated by Margaret Kenney Kress. *Southwestern Historical Quarterly* 35, no. 1 (1931).

Spann, Mrs. E., ed. *The Texian Monthly Magazine* 1, no. 1 (July 1858).

Sparks, S. F. "Recollections of S. F. Sparks." *Southwestern Historical Quarterly* 12 (1908–1909).

Spears, Patricia Lynn. *Angelina.* Austin: Eakin, 1984.

Tatum, Charles. *Shelby County.* Austin: Eakin, 1984.

Taylor, A. Elizabeth. "The Woman Suffrage Movement in Texas." *Journal of Southern History* 17 (May 1951).

Terrell, John Upton, and Donna M. Terrell. *Indian Women of the Western Morning.* Garden City, N. Y.: Anchor Press, 1976.

Texas Women's Meeting. *Summary of the Final Report to the National Commission on the Observance of International Women's Year by the Texas Coordinating Committee,* September 1977.

Thompson, Esther Lane. "The Influence of the Freedmen's Bureau on the Education of the Negro in Texas." Thesis. Texas Southern University, 1956.

Thompson, Joyce. *Marking a Trail: A History of the Texas Woman's University.* Denton: TWU Press, 1982.

Trambley, Estela Portillo. "Day of the Swallows." *El Grito* 4 (Spring 1971): 4–47.

———. *Sor Juana and Other Plays.* Ypsilanti, Mich.: Bilingual Press, 1983.

Turner, Kay. "Mexican-American Women's Home Altars." *lady-unique-inclination-of-the-night* (Autumn 1983): 71–81.

Turner, Martha Anne. *Clara Driscoll, An American Tradition.* Austin: Madrona, 1979.

———. *The Yellow Rose of Texas: Her Saga and Song.* Austin: Shoal Creek, 1976.

Upchurch, J. T. *Traps for Girls and Those Who Set Them: An Address to Men Only.* Arlington: Purity Pub., 1908.

Viele, Teresa. *Following the Drum: A Glimpse of Frontier Life.* Lincoln: University of Nebraska Press, 1984.

"W. Steinert's View of Texas in 1849 [entry for July 2, 1849]." *Southwestern Historical Quarterly* 80 (1976–1977).

Waerenskjold, Elise. *Lady with the Pen.* Edited by C. A. Clausen. Clifton: Bosque Memorial Museum, 1976.

Wallace, Patricia Ward. *A Spirit So Rare.* Austin: Nortex, 1984.

Winegarten, Ruthe. *Ann Richards, Texas State Treasurer: A Study of Her First Year in Office, 1983.* Austin: Texas Foundation for Women's Resources, 1983.

———. "The History of Women in Texas." *Texas Almanac.* Dallas: A. H. Belo Corp., 1985.

———, ed. "Cordye Hall, Texas Peacemother." Unpublished oral history. Private collection of Cordye Hall, Dallas, and Ruthe Winegarten, Austin.

———, ed. *Finder's Guide to the "Texas Women, A Celebration of History" Exhibit Archives.* Denton: Texas Woman's University, 1984.

———, ed. *I Am Annie Mae [Hunt]: The Personal Story of a Black Texas Woman.* Austin: Rosegarden Press, 1983.

———, ed. *Texas Women's History Project Bibliography.* Austin: Texas Foundation for Women's Resources, 1980.

Woloch, Nancy. *Women and the American Experience.* New York: Knopf, 1984.

Wygant, Larry J. "A Note on the Early Medical Education of Women at UTMB." *The Bookman* [Moody Medical Library], March 1980.

Young, Mary Sophie. "Journal." *Southwestern Historical Quarterly* 65, no. 3 (1961–1962).

———. *A Key to the Families and Genera of Flowering Plants and Ferns in the Vicinity of Austin, Texas.* University of Texas Bulletin, No. 1754, Sept. 25, 1917.

———. *The Seed Plants, Ferns, and Fern Allies of the Austin Region.* University of Texas Bulletin, No. 2065, Nov. 20, 1920.

Young, Maud Jeannie. *Familiar Lessons in Botany.* New York: Barnes, 1873.

Zamoro, Emilio. *Los Tejanos: Children of Two Cultures.* South Texas Head Start Bilingual-Bicultural Conference. South Texas Regional Training Office. Pan American University, Edinburg, January 5–6, 1978.

Manuscript Collections

(All locations are in Texas unless otherwise noted.)

Austin History Center. Austin Public Library. Jane Y. McCallum Collection; Elizabeth Sthreshley biography.

Barker Texas History Center. UT-Austin. Cazneau Papers; Mrs. Fannie Heartsill Papers; Neblett Papers; Pennybacker Papers.

Bexar County Archives, San Antonio. María Betancour will.

Brazoria County Historical Survey Committee. Family Records, File 25.

Dallas Historical Society. Sarah Cockrell Papers.

Duke University, Durham, N. C. Harriet Person Perry Papers.

Edna Gladney Home Archives, Ft. Worth.

Governor's Commission for Women, Austin.

Houston Metropolitan Research Center. Houston Public Library. Minnie Fisher Cunningham Collection; Anna Dupree Papers.

Institute of Texan Cultures, San Antonio. Jewish Texans File; Dolores Linton File.

Life Planning/Health Services, Dallas.

Moody Medical Library Archives. UT-Medical Branch at Galveston. Dr. Kenneth Aynesworth letter to Lillian Bedichek, 1933.

National Council of Negro Women Archives, Washington, D. C.

Plano Public Library, Plano. Elizabeth Carpenter Diary.

Southwest Collection. Texas Tech University, Lubbock. Mrs. Rowland Clyde Burns Diary.

Texas Collection. Baylor University, Waco. Bertie Barron letter; Jeffie O. A. Conner Papers; Dorothy Scarborough Collection.

Texas/Dallas History and Archives Division. Dallas Public Library. Juanita Craft Papers.

Texas PTA Archives, Austin.

Texas Women's History Project Exhibit Archives. Texas Woman's University, Denton.

INDEX

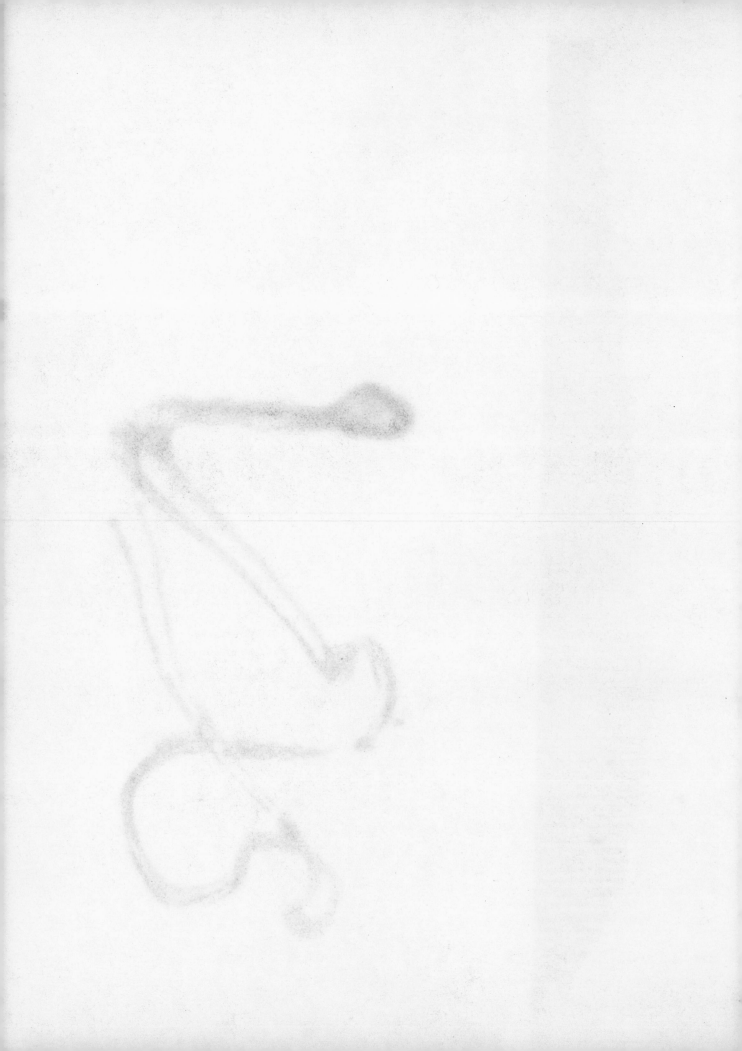

T
305.4
WIN
c1
Winegarten, Ruthe
Texas women

DATE DUE

1986

AUG 2 5

OCT

APR 1

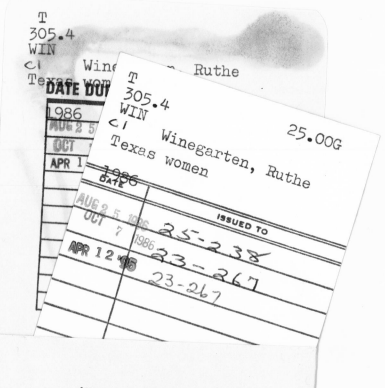

T
305.4
WIN   25.00G
c1
    Winegarten, Ruthe
Texas women

1986
DATE

AUG 2 5 1986   ISSUED TO
OCT 7 1986   25-238
APR 12 96   23-267
                23-267

VIRGIL AND JOSEPHINE GORDON
MEMORIAL LIBRARY
917 North Circle Drive
SEALY, TEXAS 77474

DEMCO